PURSUING
THE SEASONS OF GOD

PURSUING
THE SEASONS OF GOD

John Fenn

Aura Productions LLC
Hays, Kansas

ISBN (1st ed) 0-9702551-0-1

Cover Photograph by Emiko Taki
Cover Design by Aura Productions LLC
Book Design by Gennifer A Marconette
Edited by Gennifer A Marconette and Jayna Hill

Unless otherwise indicated, Scripture is quoted from the
King James Version of the Bible.

Also referenced, *Vine's Complete Expository Dictionary of
Old and New Testament Words.*
Copyright 1996 by Thomas Nelson Publishers.

The author and publisher chose not to acknowledge satan by
capitalizing his name; grammatical rules have been violated due to
this decision, but we felt it was necessary.

For information about permission to reproduce selections from this
book, write to Permissions, Aura Productions LLC,
106 West 17th St, Hays, KS 67601.

Publisher's Cataloging-in-Publication Data
Fenn, John, 1958-
    Pursuing the seasons of God / John Fenn. -- 2nd ed.
    p. cm.
    LCCN 2009922373
    ISBN-13: 978-0-9794167-4-3
    ISBN-10: 0-9794167-4-4

    1. Desire for God. 2. God (Christianity) 3. God
(Christianity)--Knowableness. 4. God (Christianity)--
Promises. 5. God (Christianity)--Will. 6. Private
revelations. 7. Christian life.   I. Title.

BV4501.3.F466 2009   248.4
                    QBI09-200029

*With thanks and love to my wife Barb,
whose spiritual strength and character
I admire so much.*

CONTENTS

INTRODUCTION

Paul said in II Corinthians 12:1: "I will come to visions and revelations of the Lord." He also writes in Ephesians 3:3: "How that by revelation he made known unto me." Paul didn't only receive insights into the written Word of God, he experienced revelations of the Lord's realm and these experiences enlightened, supplemented, reinforced, and enhanced his understanding of the scripture.

This book contains a few of the visitations from Jesus and his angels—visitations I have had pertaining to being sensitive to the timing of the Holy Spirit in our lives. I share parts of them only for the purposes of instruction and insight into the things of God, not for the sake of the experiences themselves.

It is my hope that this book may 'normalize' the heavenly realm for the reader and lead to greater sensitivity to his leading in our lives.

This is the story of how the Lord taught me to be sensitive to his realm, and helped me understand his—and heaven's—perspective of our lives in him. I pray that your own understanding of scripture will be enriched and you will be encouraged to "press toward the mark for the prize of the high calling of God in Christ Jesus."

1

Sensitive to the Spirit Realm

My eyes were closed as the congregation moved deeper into worship. My wife and I were the only ones sitting in one of the back rows of the church, and there was no one else in our row of about 12 chairs. As I was caught up in worship I turned to my right and saw Jesus walk in the back of the church, then start walking up the main aisle to the end of our row. I say I turned, meaning my spirit's head turned. Physically, I was still standing with my eyes shut and hands upraised, but within my body my spirit man's head turned and saw Jesus. He wore a long white robe and it seemed light emanated from him. It wasn't that he was lit up, but rather he was light itself.

He smiled slightly as he said, "Come with me," and motioned me toward him with his hand.

Like a cicada leaving its shell, I stepped out of my body and walked the length of the row and into the aisle of the church. He started up the aisle and I followed slightly behind and to his right. Jesus stepped in front of the front row and turned to face a Navajo pastor from the Navajo reservation in Arizona who was visiting that Sunday. Our church supported this pastor financially and groups from our church had made several trips to his church.

As I followed Jesus he stepped in front and to the side

of the pastor and motioned for me to step directly in front of him.

He said, "I have a word for him and I want you to lay hands on him." I responded, "Lord, you're here, why do I need to lay hands on him?" He replied with a smile, "Just do it." And so I said, "OK, Lord, if you say so."

His tone was so kind and patient, and I could tell he wanted to teach me something. As I laid my hands on the pastor's head I began to flow in a prophecy that encouraged him and told him how much the Lord appreciated his work and right heart. After about 20 seconds of the prophecy Jesus began to "melt" into me. He began entering into me and perfectly conformed to my form and outstretched arms. This was interesting to me because I am six feet six inches tall and he appeared to be about five feet eleven inches or six feet tall, but he "melted" perfectly into my spirit.

As he did so I heard him say, "When you lay hands on a person in my name, it is as if I am personally laying hands on them. Walk in this authority, my son." Within a few seconds the prophecy ended and suddenly I was back in my body with my eyes closed worshiping in song. I quickly opened my eyes, looked around, and realized it had all happened within the one worship song we had been singing.

Moving in Two Realms

When I was first born again, as a teenager, the more I studied the Bible the more I began to believe that Adam and Eve could operate and see in both the physical and spiritual worlds simultaneously. The Lord had made Adam's body and put him in the garden (Gen 2:15). He brought all the animals to Adam for him to name (Genesis 2:19). The Lord made Eve and brought her to Adam (Genesis 2:22), and they both heard the Lord walking in the garden (3:8). To truly be able to operate in the physical and spiritual realm at the same time became my heart's desire.

In Luke 8:46 I saw how Jesus was being grabbed at and thronged by a crowd, yet one woman who touched the hem of his clothing in faith drew healing power from him.

He said, **"I perceive that virtue** [power] **is gone out of me."**

What intrigued me wasn't the woman's faith, but rather that Jesus could, in the midst of all the commotion, be so sensitive to the spirit realm that he perceived power going from him. Jesus was able to take in information with his physical senses while at the same time he was aware what was happening in his spirit. I saw examples like this in Jesus' life and set my heart to seek the Lord and to be sensitive to my spirit while operating in the natural day-to-day routine.

Psalm 103:7 was my heart's desire: **"He made known his ways unto Moses, his acts unto the children of Israel."**

I didn't want to be like the Israelites who saw manna, water from a rock, the plagues of Egypt, and other miracles. Those were the acts of God and I saw many Christians waiting for yet another act of God to rescue them for some circumstance. I was determined to be like Moses who knew the *ways* of God. If I knew his ways then the miracles would follow. Jesus said in John 5:19 that he could do nothing of himself, but whatever he saw the Father doing, that is what he did. He said in verse 30:

"...of mine own self do nothing: as I hear, I judge."

I wanted to be as sensitive to the Father as Jesus was.

Healing School

The spring that I saw Jesus come into the church I began holding "healing school" on Monday afternoons in the church. Usually about 15-20 people would come; I would teach a little from the Bible about healing and then we would pray for one another. We would open with some worship or a time of extended prayer, and it was during those times I began seeing things in the spirit realm while my eyes were wide open.

I looked at one lady and above her head was a flame shaped like a large Aspen leaf (or Cottonwood); it was a shaped fire of light hovering over her. The base of the flames seemed to be about six feet tall or so over her head and the total height was about two feet tall. Within and all over the main "flame" were lots of little tongues of flame. I began to wonder if the "cloven tongues like as of fire" in Acts 2:3 wasn't the little single flame I had seen in Renaissance paintings, but rather these big flames I was seeing. It was silent and was the same light that I saw in Jesus when he came into the service and called me to walk up front with him.

When I saw the tongue of fire I immediately began getting words of knowledge and a prophecy for her. As that prophecy was winding down I began to see another flame over someone else and I would receive words for them. Sometimes the words were more words of wisdom and prophetic towards the future in nature, sometimes they were words of a more personal and private nature. Oftentimes they dealt with hidden fears or worries that a person was dealing with and were words of encouragement and exhortation.

There were times I would see a shaft of light that seemed to come straight through the ceiling and into a person's head. At times, there would be a cylinder of light the diameter of the person's head and they would receive words of instruction from the Lord that went straight into their spirit man. Other times the shaft was wide enough that their whole body was encased in the shaft, and in those times the person would most truly be "in the Spirit." They weren't really aware what was going on around them. It reminded me of Peter's vision in Acts 10:10 when it says he fell into a trance and saw a vision. When I would look closely at the shaft of light I could see written words from the Lord flowing down the cylinder into the person's head. Oftentimes the person would sit "frozen": hands up slightly in worship, eyes closed, totally "in the Spirit" and unaware of us. Then I would see the light fade slowly away and the person would begin writing down everything the Lord had told them, or begin weeping, or just sit quietly while they took it all in.

I saw these things while my eyes were open, and the people sitting around the circle had no idea what was going on.

Jesus Appears and Teaches Me

In the fall of that year, I took a missions trip to the Saltillo, Mexico area. The schedule called for me and a missionary named Carl to go to Laguna de Sanchez, a village in the mountains, about 2½ hours away. Another visiting American named Dora was to act as interpreter. A Mexican man from the village came to pick us up in Saltillo in his Volkswagen van and drove us up. I did not feel good that day. My head hurt and I felt nauseated, but I knew the local people were expecting a service and I had come to serve the Lord, so I drank some water, laid hands on myself in prayer, and went. It took about 90 minutes before I started to feel better, but I'm glad I went.

As we pulled into the village we saw a goat being held by several men; one of them took a sharp knife and jabbed the goat's jugular vein just as we passed. Blood started flowing like a fountain as the Mexican driver of our van told Carl that was our dinner. I steeled myself inside to keep in mind I would eat what was set before me and receive it as unto the Lord.

There were a couple of hours before dinner and the service, so Carl, Dora and I walked around the village. It was situated around a dry mountain lake, whose lakebed served as fields where the villagers raised their crops. Artesian wells flowed out of a nearby mountain and the water was carried to the valley floor by aqueducts. The little road we were on had very large rocks, so I was constantly looking down to watch where I stepped. I lagged behind in prayer and preparation for the service as Dora and Carl went ahead back into the village.

As I was walking back, I suddenly noticed that down inside me, in my spirit man, there was a very excited feeling. It was like my spirit knew something my mind did not yet know. As I continued walking up the road back into the village I came to a place where the road made a 90 degree right turn, then went straight for 50 feet or so, then made a 90 degree left turn and proceeded up the hill into the village. I had just turned right and was walking slowly along the short

50-foot stretch when I realized where I had felt that feeling of excitement in my spirit before.

I heard myself say, "That's Jesus."

When I said that I looked up to the "elbow" where the road made the 90 degree left—now only about 15 feet away— and Jesus was standing there on the road.

Light was shining out from him, and as it slowly proceeded from him it acted like a curtain spreading on all sides that covered the village and surrounding area. I looked to my left and watched Carl and Dora continue walking up the road; I remember realizing they didn't know the Lord was here and someone should tell them, just as the curtain of light obscured them from view.

Everything disappeared except me and Jesus.

Unfathomable Love

I looked into his eyes and it seemed like tangible, touchable love was pouring out. I felt like that little dog on the morning cartoons that would eat a biscuit, then hug himself and jump into the air and float down like a feather. I wanted to run to him and jump up and lay down in the love that was coming out from his eyes.

I noticed the light coming from him was pure white, but also all the colors in the spectrum at the same time. It seemed that when he moved the colors were scattered into the spectrum, and when he stood still it was pure white light. His eyes were so deep and full of love it seemed I could see through them into eternity. There was a sense of sadness and deep wisdom in his eyes, but pure life and joy at the same time. As I stared into his eyes I was receiving into my being the love that flowed out of them, and I could feel myself getting wisdom, revelation and strength as I stood there.

I immediately knew that my total being—my life, my heart, and mind were completely and totally exposed and naked before him—that he knew everything about me and every thought I had ever thought—yet I had never been so completely at peace and at ease.

In this natural world, if I want to look at the details of a leaf or flower 15 feet away, no matter how hard I look at it, I have to walk over to it and get that flower within a foot or so of my eyes to be able to see the details. As I looked into his pupils I was able—from 15 feet away—to also be right there before him looking at every detail; and when I wanted to look closer into those eyes through which all that love was pouring, I could see through his pupils into his mind and very being. It was like his eyes went on forever, they were that deep.

As I stared into this love I was pulled into his eyes. Suddenly I saw all the stars, galaxies, the black eternity of space, and was overcome with the overwhelming revelation that Jesus is the Creator of the universe. My eyes continued looking as if I had been transported through his eyes and was now traveling through space and eternity and his vast knowledge. I looked all around me and wherever I looked I saw design and plan and order.

Every galaxy, every cloud of gas and star cluster and planet—he had made them all and the presence of his love and wisdom emanated from every molecule of the universe. I realized he is there and knows it all and created it all. I was overwhelmed and in awe. I realized he held all the secrets of the universe, of life, of death, and he knew how everything and everyone was put together. It wasn't like I looked into his eyes and went out the back of his head, but rather I looked into those eyes and within them, and within his head and mind, was all eternity.

A Unique Creation

At that moment I understood that I was a product of his imagination. He had thought me up and I knew he was happy with what he had made. It wasn't that he was happy or unhappy with my life and what I was doing, it was that I, as his creation, was pleasing to him. He was pleased with what he had made.

I was created based on thoughts and designs he had spent time thinking about.

I was someone he had given thought to concerning my likes and dislikes, my sense of humor, my sense of order, my love of studying his word, and he had built me based on his love and foreknowledge. Based on those thoughts he made me be born when and where I was, and into the family I was born in. I was created exactly according to his will and purpose. I thought to myself and to him at the same time, "The fact that I like the Three Stooges, you put that in me." (I like some slapstick comedy, puns, and have a dry sense of humor.) As I contemplated these things in his presence, my questions and his answers came in rapid-fire succession: "I'm truly one of your creations. You thought me up—I am a product of your imagination."

"Yes, you are, and I love you."

"You put the same amount of time, effort, and thought into everyone who has ever lived or ever will live didn't you?"

"Yes, and I love them equally as well."

As the revelation flowed I began to think out loud,

"That's part of what you did for eternity before you made the earth: you were thinking about all of us, our personalities, our circumstances, the times we would be born and die in, how you would make us, all these things you thought of beforehand for everyone who ever has or ever will live."

He smiled a great, big smile, and the love flowing out from him seemed to increase manifold. As the depth of what I just said sunk into my understanding, I could only respond, "Oh Lord, I worship you, you are worthy of all praise and honor and worship." At that moment the words of II Timothy 1:9 came alive:

"Who hath saved us, and called us with a holy calling, not according to our works, but <u>according to his own purpose and grace which was given us in Christ Jesus before the world began</u>."

And Jeremiah 1:5 **"Before you were in your mother's womb, I knew you."**

I spoke out of part question and part revelation,

"When you made the world and called everything you had made 'good,' that's what you did when you thought us each up individually. It wasn't just that the stars were good or the trees were good or the animals were good. When each of us was complete within your mind and imagination you called each one of us 'good' and went on to create the next person, and you did this before you did anything in the creation part of the book of Genesis."

"What about people born into difficult circumstances and families, how could you do that?"

He replied, "When I created each person I placed within them the ability and strength to overcome whatever circumstances they would encounter <u>as they sought me</u>. Understand that I place the potential to overcome within everyone, but that ability requires the person to depend on me because I am the source of that ability."

I understood for the first time that he would make one person very strong in character and they would be born into circumstances that would require them to use that strength to depend on the Lord to see them through. To another he would create a person not as strong and place them in a 'softer' situation, one that was still equal to their character, but would require them to use all they had been given to depend on the Lord and draw strength from him.

I understood that from the Lord's perspective there is equality for all so that God could not be blamed come judgment day.

Then I thought about babies and innocent young children who die never having had a chance in life. I thought about starving children in parts of Africa and wondered how he could let them suffer and die like that.

He said, "They are with me" in a very upbeat, positive

tone that seemed to communicate, "Didn't you know that?"

His "they are with me" also carried with it the knowledge that he has thorough and complete knowledge of them and he has made provision for them, too, and a part of that provision is the comfort of heaven. I remembered God's sense of justice exhibited to the beggar who died, Lazarus, as told in Luke 16:19-26:

"...Son, remember that thou in thy lifetime receivedst thy good things, and likewise Lazarus evil things: but now he is comforted, and thou art tormented."

I suddenly understood that although starving children are not what he wants, to him this life is but a vapor or moment in eternity, and he takes joy in receiving the little ones who suffer on earth.

He had a perspective on eternity which made any length of suffering in this life seem exceedingly short in comparison to the plans he has for our future.

I understood that those babies and young children who died are growing up in heaven now, and many of the lowest on earth are now being gloriously cared for and exalted in heaven. Peace about the injustices of the world flowed over me. I was overwhelmed with the knowledge that he was fair and just, and in the end all will be revealed.

"Remember, everything was created by me and for me, and it is only through me that the world can be made right. All things will be made right in the end, for I am just and fair. Know that those who have died in me will have glorious opportunities in the future. Have you not read Ephesians 2:7

that says my Father has saved you that in the **ages to come** he can show you the exceeding riches of his grace?"

Heaven's Reason for Salvation

He continued: "From earth's perspective people get saved and concentrate on Ephesians 2:6, that they've been raised up and seated in the heavenly places in me. Sometimes they want the Father to deliver them from some temporary circumstance, or they sense the emptiness of their lives as they are drawn by the Spirit, but from our perspective you have been saved for verse 7, for the ages to come. The Father and I saved you for verse 7. You are in eternity right now, my son. Walk according to the higher purpose and plan for your life."

I asked him, "Why are you here?"

He replied, "I'm here to meet the needs of the people."

I responded from a state of mind much like I imagined Peter was in on the mount of transfiguration when he asked about building tents for Moses, Elijah and Jesus. I responded, "How can I help?" thinking that I would follow him around and be a helper.

He looked so kindly at me with a look that told me I already knew the answer, and said, "Meet the needs of the people," and with that he disappeared, and I was back in the natural realm.

Carl and Dora had continued to walk up the road totally oblivious to what I had just experienced. I thought about running to them to tell them, but the presence of the Lord was so strong on me, and the revelation of what I had received so awe inspiring, I wanted some time to myself to take it all in.

As I thought on these things I turned left to head up the little road into the village. There was a whitewashed wall that stretched for about 125 feet or so further up on the left, which had several doors and windows spaced along it, and I realized the wall was a common front wall with many houses and families living behind it. Into one of those doors Carl and Dora had disappeared to have dinner with our host family.

As I began walking I looked up and suddenly Jesus was standing there on the right side of the road just about 15 feet ahead of me. This time he was not in as much glory, and I could see both him and the natural world around me with my eyes open, just as I was able to see the tongues of fire and shafts of light I had seen on people earlier in the year.

Senses of the Natural Man, Senses of the Spirit Man

He told me he wanted to teach me about training my senses to discern what was happening in the spirit realm. He said that most Christians don't really follow the witness in their spirit, and many that do from time to time think that is all there is and that's as far as they go with it. He pointed out Hebrews 5:14 that says:

"Strong meat belongs to them that are of full age, even those who by reason of use have their senses exercised [trained] **to discern both good and evil."**

He said he wanted me to train my senses to be able to perceive what was happening in the spirit while being able to take in information with my physical senses at the same time.

He re-told the story of the rich man and Lazarus from Luke 16:19-26:

"There was a certain rich man, which was clothed in purple and fine linen, and fared sumptuously every day:

And there was a certain beggar named Lazarus, which was laid at his gate, full of sores,

And desiring to be fed with the crumbs which fell from the rich man's table: moreover the dogs came and licked his sores.

And it came to pass, that the beggar died, and was carried by the angels into Abraham's bosom: the rich man also died, and was buried; and in hell he lift up his eyes, being in torments, and seeth Abraham afar off, and Lazarus in his bosom.

And he cried and said, Father Abraham, have mercy on me, and send Lazarus, that he may dip the tip of his finger in water, and cool my tongue; for I am tormented in this flame.

But Abraham said, Son, remember that thou in thy lifetime receivedst thy good things, and likewise Lazarus evil things: but now he is comforted, and thou are tormented.

And beside all this, between us and you there is a great gulf fixed: so that they which would pass from hence to you cannot; neither can they pass to us, that would come from thence…"

The Lord pointed out to me that both men died, and

their bodies with their physical senses were buried up on the earth, yet in their respective places their spirits and souls each had senses.

They could still talk to one another, hear each other, see each other, feel the heat or comfort, taste the water, and in every way were as normal as when they were alive, but these were senses of the spirit realm. The root of our physical senses is in our spirit. Their physical senses had died with their bodies, but their spirit and soul retained senses. Physical senses pick up information from the physical realm; spiritual senses pick up information from the spirit realm.

He said I could train my mind to perceive what was happening in the spirit. He went back to Luke 8:46:

"And Jesus said, Somebody hath touched me: for I perceive that virtue is gone out of me."

He told me there was a huge crowd all around him with many people grabbing at him (verse 45), but he had to take in information with his physical senses and at the same time have his mind <u>also</u> on what was happening in his spirit.

Thunder, an Angel, or God?

We hurry through life, and usually our minds are so focused on the physical realm we only realize God was trying to speak to us *after* we have a quiet time to reflect on an incident or issue. It is then that our minds realize what our spirit had been sensing. Similarly, in John 12:28-30 we see varying degrees of sensitivity to the Spirit of God:

"Father, glorify thy name." Then came there a

voice from heaven, saying, "I have both glorified it, and will glorify it again."

The people therefore, that stood by, and heard it, said that it thundered: others said, An angel spake to him.

Jesus answered and said, "This voice came not because of me, but for your sakes."

There are three groups of people mentioned: Those that heard thunder, those that heard a voice but thought it was an angel, and those that heard the Father just as he had spoken.

Jesus made it clear this was the voice of the Father, but some heard only a clap of thunder! How dull of hearing we are! We go on about life totally oblivious to his voice then whine about him not talking to us. How many times has the Lord been trying to get our attention by speaking something into our spirits and we totally ignore it because we are so focused on the physical realm?

The second group realized something supernatural had happened. They heard a voice, but thought it was an angel. They could not distinguish between the Father and an angel! There are times the Lord speaks something into our spirit, and we recognize it as such, but we are dull of hearing to the extent that we don't know exactly what he is saying. We think on it, we know it's him, we sense he is trying to say something, but then we go on about our business and don't take time to spend with him so we can discover what it is he's trying to say.

The last group obviously consisted of at least Jesus and the apostle John who wrote the Gospel. They heard clearly the voice of the Father saying,

"I have both glorified it, and will glorify it again."

The other two groups didn't know anything that was said. The first group heard a thunderclap, and the other group thought it was an angel. This group was dull enough to say, **"An angel spake <u>unto him</u>."** They thought the voice spoke to Jesus, but the reality was that Jesus said <u>the voice came for them</u>!

This is also the level of sensitivity many people are at when they get a word: they recognize it is supernatural, but don't know who it is for or when they should give it. When the Lord speaks it is for our benefit, but we must be sensitive enough to be able to perceive his voice exactly as he speaks and not be ready to move until we get clarity.

The Combining of the Senses

Jesus pointed out to me how he dealt with the scribes in attendance when the man was let down through the roof in Mark 2:5-8:

"When Jesus saw their faith, he said unto the sick of the palsy, Son, thy sins be forgiven thee.
But there were certain of the scribes sitting there, and reasoning in their hearts,
Why doth this man thus speak blasphemies? Who can forgive sins but God only?
And immediately <u>when Jesus perceived in his spirit</u> that they so reasoned within themselves, he said unto them, Why reason ye these things in your hearts?

He shared how he had to take in information with his natural senses, but also was aware of the senses in his spirit. It is the combining of this information that gives us God's wisdom in the situations we encounter in life.

He saw the faith of the men demonstrated by them letting their friend down through the roof. He saw the roof being taken apart. He saw the man being lowered. He saw the reactions of everyone in the house. Then he shifted the focus of his attention on what his spirit man's senses were telling him, and through the Holy Spirit's information being communicated to his spirit, he perceived the scribes' thoughts.

He said that in many cases in the New Testament, the words 'perceive' and 'discern' refer to the action of picking up in your mind the information your spirit man is receiving from the Holy Spirit, and the process through which the mind discerns which action to take.

He next told me about Paul in Acts 14:8-10:

"And there was a certain man at Lystra, impotent in his feet, being a cripple from his mother's womb, who never had walked:
The same heard Paul speak: who <u>steadfastly beholding him, and perceiving that he had faith</u> to be healed, Said with a loud voice, Stand upright on thy feet. And he leaped and walked."

Paul was ministering to many people, but when he looked around and his eyes fell on this man as he ministered, his mind simultaneously picked up information his spirit was telling him.

He pointed out that it was a process for Paul.

As Paul spoke he looked around and then came back to this man, made a mental note of that sense in his spirit that there was something more there, and looked over the people again. At some point Paul fixed his eyes on the man "steadfastly beholding him" and it was there that the 'perceiving he had faith to be healed' took place.

Paul had to lock his physical senses on the man in order to also fix his attention on what his spirit was telling him.

This is what first happened to me when I started seeing tongues of fire and shafts of light on people. When I first noticed it I kept on looking around at people when I taught or prayed, but when I steadfastly looked at the person I began receiving revelation in my spirit about them, either words of knowledge, wisdom, prophecy, or about healing. Though I still occasionally see tongues of fire or shafts of light on a person, most of the time when I'm ministering now I can look at a person and if there is information the Holy Spirit is telling my spirit I have trained my senses to discern that, and it immediately gets my attention.

Focusing on the Spirit Realm

I was ministering one time to a group of about 225 people, and off to my left, in the very back row, I perceived in my spirit the presence of the Lord on one lady in particular.

In my eye contact with the crowd I began speaking to that one section, and then I would look away at the people in the other sections, then look back at her as part of that section, then look around again.

As I began to focus my attention on that section and her in particular, suddenly I saw an angel standing behind her with his hands on her shoulders. As I 'steadfastly' looked at this, the angel began telling me what she was going through.

She was a single lady who had been dating a Christian man she planned on marrying, and had just discovered she was pregnant. She felt all the guilt and shame associated with her 'secret' and didn't see how the Lord could forgive her.

The angel was telling her how much the Lord loved her and how he forgave her and told her to do what was right, not what was convenient, but to deal with it. I spoke to her as I ministered and shared with her the part about how the Lord loved her and was with her, withholding for privacy sake the more personal information. In that way she was able to receive the peace that was the object of the angel's mission.

Later I had the opportunity to talk to her privately; she confirmed everything, and I was able to share the rest of the information, which gave her greater peace. She and her boyfriend are now married and active in ministry. I would have missed the Lord entirely if my mind didn't first notice and then be willing to focus on what my spiritual senses were telling me.

Judging Correctly

I Corinthians 2:9-16 teaches us part of the process of receiving natural information and spiritual information at the same time:

"Eye hath not seen, nor ear heard, neither have entered into the heart of man, the things which God hath prepared for them that love him.

But God hath revealed them unto us by his Spirit: for the Spirit searcheth all things, yea, the deep things of God.

Even so the things of God knoweth no man, but the Spirit of God.

Now we have received, not the spirit of the world, but the spirit which is of God; that we might know the things that are freely given to us of God.

But the natural man receiveth not the things of the Spirit of God: for they are foolishness unto him: neither can he know them, because <u>they are spiritually discerned.</u>

But he that is spiritual <u>judgeth</u> all things, yet he himself is judged of no man.

For who hath known the mind of the Lord, that he may instruct him? But we have the mind of Christ."

The Greek word translated "**discerned**" in verse 14 is the same word translated "**judgeth**" in verse 15. It means 'discern, distinguish, separate out so as to investigate, or judge' (Vine's).

That is to say, "**...they are spiritually discerned, distinguished, separated out so as to investigate. But he that is spiritual discerns, distinguishes, separates out so as to investigate all things...**"

This is what Jesus did when he was touched by many, but he perceived one woman with faith drawing healing power from him.

This is what Paul did when he steadfastly looked at the lame man and perceived the man had faith to be healed. This is what you and I must do to truly walk in the realm in which Jesus said:

"...The son can do nothing of himself, but what he sees the Father do, for what things he does, so also does the Son."

The things God has prepared for us are revealed by the Holy Spirit and must be discerned, which is the process by which the mind of a person realizes God is speaking to him in his spirit.

The whole mind of Christ is in our spirit man, but that mind of Christ cannot be received through our physical, natural senses of sight, hearing, and imagination. But we can receive this wisdom in our spirits, and in accordance with Hebrews 5:14b:

"...who by reason of use have their senses trained [exercised] **to discern both good and evil."**

The word "discern" in this text is the Greek word "diakrisis." According to Vine's Dictionary of New Testament Words it means, "a distinguishing, a clear discrimination, discerning, judging."

Hebrews 5:14b could be translated:

"...who by reason of use have their senses exercised and trained to distinguish, make a clear discrimination and judgment between good and evil."

It is this daily and continual practice of training the mind to shift attention to what is happening in our spirit man that is the key to walking in sensitivity to the Spirit.

It's our human—<u>natural</u>—nature to be focused on what our physical senses are telling us, but even before we were born again many of us have had our spirit man's senses telling us not to enter into a relationship, or we 'just feel right' about a particular job. The spirit man is still eternal—lost, but still eternal before a person is born again—but it takes the life of the Spirit of God to bring our spirit into the things of God.

Jesus reminded me about a certain store my wife and I had gone to in the mall in the town where we lived, and how each of us sensed something demonic and of an eastern religious spirit there.

We had walked in just looking for a gift, but from what we saw with our eyes we could tell there were many eastern religion items for sale. The jewelry, knick-knacks, pictures and other things all indicated eastern religion, and Buddhism in particular.

The information we took in with our physical sense of sight caused our attention to shift to how our spirits felt being in there, and we realized the feeling in our spirits was an uneasiness, a sense that deception was present, even a seducing feeling. In reminding me of this, Jesus pointed out that we had taken in information in the natural and then shifted our minds' attention to how it felt in the spirit man, and realized the spirit present was of Buddhism.

You see, each element of the spirit realm has its own "feel" in the spirit. Spirits of lust, religion, depression, and the entire evil realm give off particular 'feelings' or witness in the spirit, just as different objects and items in the natural look and feel and taste differently. We had learned that each realm of satan gave off a particular witness in our spirits, and we made a point of remembering what each witness felt like, and put it away in our memory so that we would remember that feeling.

One of the biggest keys to moving in this level of sensitivity to the Spirit of God is remembering what each witness feels like and making a point of thinking enough about it so when you come across that feeling in your spirit in the future you will recall what it is. I don't know how many times my wife and I have met someone who gave us a funny feeling in our spirits and then discussed what it was and where we had felt it before and were able to pinpoint where that person was spiritually.

As Jesus and I stood there talking, he changed the subject and moved away from the teaching to begin sharing his heart quite openly. He greatly desires to be with his children in close fellowship and to be personally involved in all our lives, as a close friend would be.

He said that he longed for his people to walk with him in this level of intimacy, but expressed sadness that so many were caught up in the world, and relatively few really set their hearts to walk in the Spirit.

He exhorted me to learn to discipline my mind to be aware of both the natural and spiritual realms at the same time. It is a discipline to train your mind to constantly be in "search" mode shifting attention between the natural world's senses and the spirit man's realm. It is through this 'reason of use' process that the senses' ability to discern between good and evil is realized.

After this teaching he said he would give me some training, then he disappeared. I walked a little way up the path and suddenly he re-appeared again to my left and about 15 feet away. He made me stop and notice that I was seeing the natural things around me and had first sensed in my spirit where he was; when I concentrated on the spirit man's senses that realm became predominant and he became clear.

It was like a game of hide and seek: He disappeared again, then I sensed where I first felt a concentration of his presence, then when I steadfastly looked at that area he was visible to me, this time on the right side about 15 feet away.

He pointed out that the more I concentrated my attention on where I sensed his presence was, the more aware of him I became.

He said that when a person moves in the gifts of the Spirit it is the same process: they perceive a word is forming or coming forth in their spirit, but it often begins as something vague. They must also be aware of the natural realm, the order of service, the teamwork with others in the service, all the while sensing the right timing and words in the spirit realm as they become more clear in the spirit man.

Most people only look for the gifts in a service where the corporate faith and atmosphere is conducive to perceiving the things of God. It is those situations that are the easiest to hear his voice. Most people who move in the gifts stop here and never really analyze how they do it. The goal is to be like Jesus, who was sensitive when he was out among the people!

This dual attention to the natural and spiritual is what Jesus did in the gospels and what led to many manifestations of the gifts of the Spirit.

This is very different from "visualizing" Jesus or trying to force the gifts to work, or imagining him to be somewhere. He pointed out that some have picked up on some valid ways the Spirit initiates these things, then had gotten into the flesh by taking what was spirit and Holy Spirit initiated, and turned it into a method of visualization and man initiated, which, he said, is error. We can train ourselves to passively switch attention from the natural realm to the spirit realm, but manifestations of Jesus and the things of the Spirit are God initiated, not man initiated. The Holy Spirit is the one who communicates the things of God to our spirit.

To take things of the spirit and try to make something happen without the Holy Spirit's initiation can lead to much error.

Two Examples of Insensitivity

Years later I was in a service, sitting toward the back, when in the midst of the worship I suddenly saw Jesus in the aisle up near the front rows. He began just to the side of the platform and would go over and lay hands on a person and speak an encouraging word, then move on to another, working his way from the front to the back. Sometimes he would just put a hand on their shoulder and talk to them, for others he would lay his hands on either side of their face or upon their head.

I just watched him for a few minutes as he made his way toward the back where I was sitting. When he got to within about 40 feet of me he looked up, turned to me, and said:

"True worship is taking place tonight."

It seemed that the people in the front 15 or so rows were caught up in worship, but the involvement lessened the further from the front the people were, and it evidently affected how well he was able to minister to the people, as well as how well they were able to receive from him.

As he continued to walk back to where I was, he continued laying hands on people and speaking to them while keeping up a running conversation with me. He continued, "But many don't even realize I'm here tonight."

With that statement he moved towards me and paused briefly next to the man in front of me, who was busy whispering to his wife and couldn't seem to get settled.

He stood there looking at the man with his hands relaxed and folded in front of him for about 30 seconds, not saying anything, just observing. Finally, I asked him if he was going to say something to him. He turned to me and said:

"I want to tell him many things, but I can't because he has not prepared his heart to receive, and he won't enter into the flow of the Spirit in the service. But I am faithful. If he sets his heart to receive from me at a later time, as he reads my Word at home, or another service, or in private meditation on the things of the Spirit, at those times I could speak to him. This is how I must be oftentimes with my children."

"Sadly, most of this man's spiritual life consists of a service like this. In times past I have tried to talk to him about certain things, for there are many questions he has for me: he is looking for direction in his work—because he is not happy there—and also for his family. He has not truly prepared himself to receive from me. The wisdom he asks of me hasn't been a high enough priority for him, though I am ready to speak to him."

I recalled the times I had perceived in my spirit that He was trying to tell me something, but was too busy to make time. Then a week or two later what he was trying to show me would become clear. "Sorry, Lord," I said. Then he smiled and said:

"It is forgiven."

I then asked about the man because he did have a bible lying on the chair next to him. "He brings it, but outside of a service, he rarely reads it for anything more than casual reading. Sometimes he'll pick it up to read, but he hasn't learned to receive from me on a personal level, so he gets bored and puts it down, though he has known me for some time. Years, in fact. If he would just fellowship with me and linger in my presence, he would receive."

The Second Example

One time I was in a large convention, sitting on the front row in a Tuesday night service. For the past several weeks I had been thinking about healing from accidents or injury and whether they were really covered by Jesus' sacrifice. I knew they had to be, but I was looking for wisdom in this area, as well as proof in the Bible that they were covered. As a minister was praying for healing for several people, I noticed that many of them had been healed of injuries sustained in car wrecks and accidents around work and the home. Suddenly I saw my angel off to my right about eight feet. When I noticed him he said:

"Much of what Jesus healed was injury."

I thought on that word for part of the night and I wondered where that fit into "himself took our infirmities and bare our sicknesses" (Matthew 8:17). I tried to remember injuries being healed in the gospels and Acts, but soon got distracted with the happenings in the service and went on to other things.

This revelation was especially important to our family because of our son with Cerebral Palsy. The lack of oxygen at birth had killed part of his brain cells, which left him mentally retarded and with multiple handicaps. But after that night I was very busy, and for the most part forgot about it the rest of the week. I thought I'd study it out after the meetings in a week or two.

On Saturday night of that week there was a wonderful concert and the presence of the Lord filled the arena. I was sitting on the floor area with my oldest son in his wheelchair next to me. Suddenly my spirit felt that familiar presence of Jesus Himself enter the arena. As I sat there looking at the stage, he walked up to me from behind and stood just to the left of my left shoulder. I glanced down to see his feet and robe but didn't want to turn around since I was the only one who saw him, so I just kept looking towards the stage.

He began, "The healing of an injury usually requires the person to move the limb or part of the body that has been injured. The physical therapies operate in an element of this in that they make the limb or part of the body move as it once had."

He then told me about Matthew 15:30-31 where, among others, the lame and <u>maimed</u> were made whole. He also spoke about the man with the withered hand, the man Paul raised from the dead who had fallen out the window, and other injuries.

When he was finished I asked him why he didn't begin with a greeting or introduction, but seemed to pick up tonight where the angel had left off on Tuesday without missing a beat. He said:

"I've been trying to talk to you about this since that night, but you have been too busy to listen. Tonight was the first opportunity you gave me to continue to speak to you about it." After that he started walking around the crowd laying hands on people and speaking things to them.

Both of the above demonstrate insensitivity to the things of the Spirit of God. First was the man who rarely opens his Bible or prays while the Lord is trying to give him the answers he seeks, then myself receiving a word from the Lord and not giving it the priority I should have—to dwell on it and place myself in a position to receive the rest of it.

Training Ground

The basic elements of what I am talking about begin before a person is born again. It begins when a person first notices a tug on their spirit to get right with God. There comes a point where their mind senses the emptiness of their spirit—that there must be something more—and they (natural man and senses) discern there is something lacking spiritually. They answer that call and are born again. Again, this is Holy Spirit initiated. None of us just decided to be born again, we were drawn to the Father by the Spirit, our natural senses picked up on the condition of our spirit man, and we answered the call, believing on Jesus.

One of the first training grounds most of us encounter after we're born again involves entering into a service and learning to shut off the distractions and bustle of the process of getting to church, which are in the natural sense realm, and enter into the praise and worship service, which are of the spirit.

I remember when my wife and I were dating as teenagers and we would get ready to go to the Saturday night meeting we attended. So often it seemed that either she or I was in a bad mood. Maybe she was late, which made me grumpy, or I had done something earlier that she was angry about. For a few times we went to the service angry at each other, but then we realized that satan was using strife to keep us from receiving from God. From that point on if we didn't resolve the issue by the time we drove into the parking lot we would sit in the car until we did.

Very quickly we realized it didn't matter who was right or wrong, it only mattered that there was peace between us. Then we would tell the spirit of strife to leave, forgive each other, pray together, and then go into the service full of the joy of the Lord. We learned to shut off the natural realm and its senses in this way, and we could therefore concentrate on spiritual things and receive them.

After telling me about the man just in front of me, Jesus moved on to me and a friend of our family, who was standing next to me. He reached over and laid a hand on her and spoke some things to her, then spoke some instructions to me, then continued toward the back and around that section of chairs. Our friend started crying and she said, "Jesus was here," though she didn't see him.

The point is that she sensed his presence and received because she was flowing in the Spirit. How many of us come to a service to be observers and not participants!

While I stood there in that little village in Mexico being trained by Jesus, he waited for me to see him, receive a little more teaching, then disappeared again. Again I had a moment or two to think and walk, and again he suddenly appeared, this time to the left again, and again about 15 feet or so in front of me.

He laughed and smiled now as I was catching on to the idea of keeping my mind aware of the spirit realm and natural realm at the same time, and seeing in both at the same time. About five years earlier he told me I was called to be a seer, but I hadn't realized the full ramifications of the word until that moment. Certainly there is more involved, but it was this aspect of operating in the Spirit that answered my heart's desire.

He was having fun training me.

He enjoyed watching me as I zigzagged up the road towards him while he appeared, taught me, then disappeared, only to re-appear on up the road. The last time he reappeared on the left side and we began walking together. He was on my left as we began walking along the wall of doors and windows, and I still had no idea into which door Carl and Dora had entered.

As we walked I looked at him on my left and I thought, "I'm taller than the King of the universe." Now, there's only so far in the flesh you can go while in the spirit and in his presence, but this was an honest thought that just came into my mind.

Instantly he smiled and I realized he knew exactly what I had just thought. I said to myself, "Dummy, he knows your thoughts!" He didn't say anything, but smiled without looking at me; at that moment we arrived at a door and he paused, motioning with his left hand toward the door. With a knowing smile he said, "This is it." I crossed in front of him and went inside, and he went behind me as I entered the room.

Carl and Dora were inside sipping soft drinks with our hostess, who was making a kind of stew from the goat we had seen earlier. She served homemade tortillas with the goat stew, and I made sure I had two helpings. After the meal Carl, Dora, and I were sitting around the table talking when suddenly I sensed something in my spirit. Carl was on my left and Dora was across the table from me, sitting in a chair that was directly in front of a doorway that led to another room.

In the doorway I saw an angel standing just behind Dora. This was the first time I had seen an angel. He didn't have wings and he looked like a man in his mid 20's or so, clothed in a white robe. I began teaching her as the Lord had just been teaching me the previous 40 minutes or so.

I asked her if she sensed anything in her spirit. She said that she didn't, so I asked her to close her eyes and pray in the spirit. When she did this she said she sensed the presence of the Lord, like someone was in the room. It was amazing to me to watch her go through the same process I had just gone through. I realized we are so used to operating in the natural realm that the subtleties of the <u>spirit</u> man are often not even noticed by our <u>natural</u> man.

When she closed her eyes it shut off, for the most part, her physical senses, leaving her to be able to concentrate on her spirit man. In the same way that it is sometimes easier to give a prophecy or tongue and interpretation with the eyes closed, it's easier to concentrate on the things of the Spirit that way.

When she did this and noticed the presence of someone in the room I asked her if she could tell where he was standing. At first she couldn't, but then as she had her eyes closed she kind of 'scanned' the room with her head moving slowly from her right to left as she 'looked' around with her eyes closed, all the while sensing what her spirit was telling her.

She suddenly stopped and said, "He's right behind me."

I asked her if she could tell who it was, and she said it didn't bear witness that it was Jesus: the feeling of his presence wasn't that strong and it seemed to be *of* the Lord, but a separate individual.

She suddenly realized, "It's an angel!" and opened her eyes.

At the moment of recognition the angel moved around her and towards me and seemed to head out the door to the street which was just behind me. As I took another sip of the soft drink I thought this over.

I heard in my right ear, "Jesus is walking the streets of the village."

I thought on what I had just heard for about three seconds until I came to myself and realized what had just happened. Immediately I turned and looked over my right shoulder out the door and saw only the robed legs of the angel pass out of view as he walked up the street.

I called for Dora to follow me and we stepped outside into the street. The road continued uphill slightly into town, where it made a T. The right hand turn was 90 degrees and headed towards the church and the main part of the village. The left part of the T was more of a 45-degree turn and was actually more of a Y.

When we stepped into the street I immediately saw Jesus standing right in the middle of this intersection.

The angel that was in the kitchen behind Dora was standing about 50 feet down the Y portion of the left side. The Lord told me to continue to train Dora in what He had taught me. I asked her if she sensed anything and again she couldn't, so again I had her close her eyes. Immediately she could sense two people with the presence of the Lord. She said one was straight ahead and the other was to her left and a little further away. The one straight ahead had a stronger presence of the Lord. As we began walking with her alternating between eyes open and eyes closed, she began heading straight for Jesus, but she couldn't tell yet that it was him.

As he taught me, I taught her over a period of about 20 minutes, and we ended up with her walking with eyes closed to within 5 feet of the Lord. At that moment she suddenly opened her eyes wide and exclaimed:

"It's Jesus! And the other one is an angel."

At that, Jesus laughed so hard he bent over and put his hands on his knees, then began walking to our right and headed into the village.

She told me "he's walking away now, to his left," and with that he disappeared after about 25 feet.

After the service that night we began loading into the VW van that had brought us to the village. As I set my hand on the door to the front passenger seat I had a déjà vu experience.

I suddenly remembered a spiritual dream I had over two months earlier. I dreamed I was in a strange vehicle with a driver I didn't know and didn't speak my language, with two people on a bench seat behind me that I barely knew, and several people in the very back I didn't know at all. As we traveled down a dark, gravel mountain road we went wide on a left hand curve and rolled, coming to rest with the van on its side and my right arm partially pinned. I was able to get my arm free and realized I was the least hurt in the van. Then I woke up.

I took authority over that event and asked the Lord to protect me and send his angels to keep it from happening, then forgot about it...until the moment I put my hand on the door.

I told Dora briefly about it and she said she had a dream two days before about an accident. We forbade satan from bringing that to pass, asked the Father for his angelic protection, and got into the van.

That was one of the biggest acts of faith in my life. I truly made a decision right there that the name of Jesus was the most powerful name in the universe and I would rest in what I had just prayed, believing it had been answered.

About 15 minutes into the trip down the mountain I was looking out the front window into the darkness, and suddenly I saw first one, then a second angel descend to the point where the headlight beams stopped and the darkness began.

They descended from above and to the right and stood about 10 to 12 inches or so off the ground at the point where the beams ended. They weren't walking or running, just standing there talking to one another.

I looked over at the speedometer and realized our speed varied between 30 and 55 mph coming down the mountain, yet they remained standing perfectly relaxed 10 to 12 inches off the ground and talking between themselves, moving in perfect unison with the van.

As I observed them I could tell they were talking in some foreign language and I had the sense that they knew each other but had not seen each other in quite awhile and didn't get a chance to work together much at all. I thought that made sense if one of them was Dora's angel and the other was mine, since I didn't know her before this trip and she was from another state. It seemed natural that the angels wouldn't have the opportunity to work together because of these things. I prayed to the Lord that he would open Dora's eyes to either confirm what I was seeing or bring me back to reality!

I called back to Dora who was sitting on the bench seat behind the driver and asked her to look out the window.

Immediately she said she saw two angels and described them just as I was seeing them. Shortly thereafter we saw a third angel join them and Dora called it out the same time I did. We then asked Carl to look out front and see if he saw anything and he said he saw three angels and described them the same way.

Up until this point Carl had been holding a conversation with our driver's wife and kids who were in the very back of the van, and Dora and I had been speaking in fairly hushed tones, so when he confirmed what we were seeing we rejoiced. About that time both Dora and I suddenly realized we were coming to the place where we had each dreamed there was a wreck.

We each called out the curve at the same time. I can honestly say that I was a little nervous when we passed that curve, but nothing happened. From that point on it was fun watching the angels stand and talk. I continued training myself as Jesus had taught me and could see when the road was going to curve to the right or left even though it was totally dark. I did this by watching the angels. Before a curve they would move ahead of the headlight beams and sometimes disappear around a mountainside as the road went left or right, so I began telling Dora which way the road would curve depending on which way the angels would take off. When the van got to where they were and the headlight beams met them, instantly they were traveling at whatever speed we were going.

When they went ahead of us they didn't walk or run, they just stayed talking in a group about 10 to 12 inches above the ground but accelerated quickly and to the right or left, depending on the curve of the road.

Though I could see them accelerate and curve left or right, once they went around a mountainside I couldn't see them until we came around the curve enough. They would always be standing there, talking, and not even look up at us as we approached. What a sight to see three robed men in God's white light hovering in the darkness! After about 90 minutes of this we came out of the mountains and onto the main road, and the angels disappeared at the point the pavement began and straightened out.

2

Moving with Heaven's Timing

I was lying in bed one night with my wife asleep beside me. Earlier I had been up praying and now was just thinking on the things of the Lord. Suddenly I sensed in my spirit an angel was in the room and then, as Jesus had taught me, I gave my spiritual 'senses' attention and suddenly my eyes were opened to see him standing at the end of my bed.

He said, "It has been given to me to appear to you and speak with you. As you continue to walk in the things of the Lord it will become normal to speak with me."

His voice had a familiar ring to it but I was a bit nervous talking with an angel who just appeared in my darkened bedroom at 11 p.m!

I said, "Don't I know you? You sound familiar."

He said, "I am the one who spoke to you when you were a teenager and had the mini-bike wreck. I told you to obey your mother and put on your helmet."

Instantly I knew that was it! When I was 14, and before I knew the Lord, a friend had asked me to come over to his neighborhood on my mini-bike and race his go-cart. My mini-bike was like a small motorcycle and could go about 40 mph. As I was getting ready to go to his house I started to put on my helmet but hesitated.

I knew it wasn't "cool" to wear a helmet and he wouldn't be wearing one, but mom had made it a rule that if I wanted to ride I would have to wear the helmet.

As I hesitated I heard a voice to my right and behind me say, "Obey your mother and put on your helmet." I thought, "I think I'll obey mom and put on my helmet."

I realized as he was telling me this event from his perspective that there had been many times he spoke as a suggestion and I didn't even realize it, and just took it and made it my own 'suggestion' to myself.

A few minutes after I arrived at my friend's house I was involved in a terrible accident when my friend's go-cart slammed into my mini-bike as we were racing at 40 mph. I was knocked unconscious, woke up in the hospital, and sustained a severe concussion. I was in the hospital for three days and at home another week. To this day my memory of the event is only scrambled bits and pieces, but I know the helmet saved my life. Heaven's timing was to put my helmet on before I went to my friend's house, even though it wasn't what a teenage boy wanted to do.

My obedience saved my life.

He continued, "I was also the one who arranged for your car to slide between the fence posts when you were coming home that night on Valmont road. Satan wanted to roll the car and kill you, but I prevented it from happening."

That event happened one night when I was coming home very late and hit a patch of black ice on a bridge. The car spun around into the oncoming lane and slid backwards and sideways down an embankment into a field. The car came to rest right between two T-posts that had no wire between them. When it stopped moving I noticed one post just six inches from the front bumper and another post about six inches from my back bumper with the car neatly placed between them. I remember thanking the Lord for his protection and sat for a little bit trying to figure out what to do, but finally zigzagged the car back and forth in tiny movements until I worked it from between the posts, drove through the grassy field, up the embankment where it was less of a slope, and continued home. He told me he was surprised it took me so long to figure out how to drive out.

He said he was also the angel I saw in Mexico behind Dora—the one who had spoken to me that "Jesus is walking the streets of the village." He was the one at the Y part of the road and one of the angels in the headlight beam.

Suddenly I looked at this angel like he was an old friend. I realized he had been with me in many difficult times and his voice and presence were things I realized on a sub-conscious level at several times throughout my life, but only now did I fully understand how involved he had truly been. Now I realized he had been there at various times trying to get me to move in unison with heaven's will and timing. His voice had only been "thunder" to me before; but now I recognized it for what it truly was!

I asked him what it was like serving us, men, who are now inferior, but will one day be in charge of angels.

"We don't understand the way people move in faith. It's amazing to us that people will—just on a word or a leading in their spirit from God—pick up their whole lives and their families and move all the way across the country, or all the way around the world for the Lord, whom they've never seen."

"We're before the throne. All we know is heaven. When we take action to prepare things for you, we do it at the command of the Lord and we see him and it all the way through, so we know it's coming to pass. The way that people—living in the natural realm—never having seen our realm, will rearrange their whole lives and move out for God at His will is amazing to us. Even the day to day leadings from the Spirit and the way people live by faith are mysteries to us."

For the first time I realized the meaning of I Peter 1:12b: **"...which things the angels desire to look into."**

The angels are amazed that we will believe so surely and completely a leading from the Spirit and do things in our lives having not seen the things of God. They are charged with helping us move in heaven's timing, but they don't understand our ability to walk in both the natural and supernatural realms at the same time.

In the same way that we live in the natural world and only have glimpses of the heavenly, in like manner they live in the heavenly and only rarely do they personally touch the natural.

They see our natural lives and understand we are in this realm, but they don't understand it. To them, heaven is more real than earth. I could see that the Father and Jesus are so appreciative and have such rewards for us when we do this, because they are from the angelic perspective, too. When God speaks, it happens, and that you and I on enemy territory will follow him, having not seen him, is appreciated and rewarded by the Lord.

We need to realize that when we are willing to walk by faith—move according to knowledge from heaven's realm—we sometimes are led to do things which are contrary to what our natural senses are telling us is the right timing. But if we are moving in heaven's timing the provision has been sent ahead.

That doesn't mean we throw out common sense, but rather we must live our lives according to a higher knowledge and purpose. We must be like Moses who **"endured, as seeing him who is invisible."** (Hebrews 11:27) Moses was sensitive to both the natural and spiritual realms at the same time.

We must move according to heaven's timing, not earth's. I didn't feel that it was heaven's timing to put my helmet on, but it was. Peter may not have gotten up that morning and felt it was heaven's timing to leave fishing and follow Jesus, but it was. Matthew may not have gotten up that morning and felt like it was heaven's timing to leave the money changing profession that day, but when the call came from heaven, he acted. The rich young ruler didn't feel it was heaven's timing to sell everything, but it was, even though he chose not to obey. He missed heaven's timing and the provision and reward that go with it.

In Luke 19:44 Jesus wept over Jerusalem and prophesied of the destruction of the city which took place nearly 40 years later in 70 AD. He said it would happen:

"...because thou knewest not the time of thy visitation."

He said in verse 42:

"If thou hadst known, at least in this thy day, the things which belong unto thy peace! But now they are hid from thine eyes."

The result of not realizing heaven's timing, or, in Jesus' words, not knowing the time of your visitation, is first of all an ignorance of what really belongs to you—**"the things which belong unto thy peace (belong to you)."**

Then, as a result of not knowing, blindness to the plan of God happens! The first step is not realizing the time of visitation. We must be sensitive to those times the Lord wants to speak to us.

Late one night I finally gave into the urge to get out of bed and go pray in the living room. For about three nights I had felt the urge in my spirit to either stay up late and pray or get out of bed. When I finally obeyed one of the first things the Lord told me was that he had been trying to talk to me for several days.

I had known I had a "divine appointment," but refused it. If I had continued to ignore the Lord's voice it could have dimmed my ability to hear him in the future. The sad part is that Israel, too, could have known the time of their visitation! They could have received God's provision: Jesus their Messiah! The result of not recognizing heaven's timing was tragic.

In Israel's case, we are told in Romans 11:25:

"...that blindness in part is happened to Israel"

Blindness concerning the fact that Jesus is their Messiah! We must realize the time of our visitation, and then we will know what belongs to us!

Jesus always moved with a sense of heaven's timing. He fashioned his natural earthly schedule around heaven's schedule and timetable. In Luke 9:31 at the transfiguration, Moses and Elijah appear in glory to speak with him:

"..of his decease [death] **which he should accomplish at Jerusalem."**

Moses represents the law and was able to speak to Jesus of the Old Testament types and shadows of the suffering he would have to undergo, while Elijah, who represents all prophecy, was able to share with him what had been prophesied. The purpose was to inform and direct Jesus to heaven's appointment at the cross.

After this revelation of heaven's timing, the whole tone and attitude of Jesus' life and ministry changed. Verse 41:

"O faithless and perverse generation, how long shall I be with you…"

And verse 44:

"Let these sayings sink down into your ears: for the Son of man shall be delivered into the hands of men."

In verse 51, he **"set his face to go to Jerusalem."**

And in chapter 10, he sends out the seventy. When we know it is heaven's timing to act, we must have the same determination to see it come to pass that Jesus had. He stayed focused and made plans for his departure by sending forth the seventy.

Has the Revelation, Missed the Timing

Moses is an example of someone who had heaven's plan but tried to apply it in earth's timing. We have the idea of Moses killing one of the Egyptians and then fleeing in exile, not understanding what was going on until his burning bush experience forty years later. Nothing could be further from the truth. Acts 7:23-25:

"And when he was full forty years old, it came into his heart to visit his brethren the children of Israel.
And seeing one of them suffer wrong, he defended him, and avenged him that was oppressed, and smote the Egyptian:
For he supposed his brethren would have understood how that God by his hand would deliver them: but they understood not."

Moses killed the Egyptian knowing that he was the deliverer! He supposed his brethren had the same revelation he had, but they did not. Many people have made the same mistake Moses made regarding the sharing of a heavenly purpose and call to people who haven't received that same revelation about them. The result is rejection.

I remember when I shared with my mother-in-law that I was called into the ministry. Her response: "Why would you want to do that? There's no money in that!" I supposed she would have understood 'how that God by my hand' would lead her daughter into marriage and the ministry. How wrong I was!

There are times to keep such revelations to ourselves until God backs up our claims with signs following. In this case the signs following included a stable marriage and strong family life when other family members underwent various life-changing tragedies. But in His time He confirmed my call and our marriage to my in-laws.

Moses was trained in the ways of the Egyptians, and the historian Josephus tells us he was a military leader as well. It is evident that when Moses killed the Egyptian **"he supposed his brethren would have understood"** he was the deliverer, and he figured God would use his natural training to cause Israel to rise in civil war and defeat the Egyptians.

This mistake cost him forty years in the wilderness. It is a mistake to think we will "help" God fulfill his vision for our lives.

He doesn't need our fleshly help, thank you! Moses had to learn the way God would deliver them wasn't through his military training and revolt, but rather through the supernatural working of miracles!

The way God chose to deliver them hadn't even entered into Moses' mind when he received the revelation that he was the deliverer. He made the mistake of mixing a God-given vision with his own plans assuming he knew how it would happen. But with God, it's his vision, his plan, and his methods of fulfilling them! Moses should have waited and gone about his business, keeping this revelation inside himself until heaven's timing was revealed.

Moses had the right vision from God, but he took the timing into his own hands. But even though he missed the timing, he still retained the revelation of his call within himself. Hebrews 11:27 tells us that:

"by faith he forsook Egypt."

This means even though he knew he had missed it, he held onto his vision. Imagine leaving your homeland after you missed God's timing and going into the wilderness <u>in faith and confidence!</u>

"For he endured [persevered]**, as seeing him who is invisible."**

He was confident he had the vision, and he knew he had missed the timing.

The Lord shares with us bits and pieces about our vision and his timing, but it is walking through it step by step in unison with the Holy Spirit that puts all the pieces together. There are three separate, and apparently unrelated, promises about the Messiah in Matthew 2:

V 4-6 **"...he demanded of them where Christ should be born. And they said unto him, In Bethlehem of Judea: for thus it is written by the prophet..."**

V 15 **"...that it might be fulfilled which was spoken of the Lord by the prophet, saying, Out of Egypt have I called my son."**

V 23 **"...and dwelt in a city called Nazareth: that it might be fulfilled which was spoken by the prophets, he shall be called a Nazarene."**

These are three words of promise about where the Messiah will be from, but it took the event actually happening before man was able to make sense of them.

They say the Christ will be from Bethlehem, Egypt, and Nazareth. If you and I were living in that time, how would we be able to have the wisdom to understand the timing of their fulfillment? We wouldn't. The Lord still does this type of thing today to you and I.

One young lady came to me confused: "I feel like the Lord is telling me I'm going to go overseas to a mission base, but I'm supposed to go to another year of school, and he's also leading me to work in the nursery. Is this God?"

Of course! It's just a matter of timing and obedience to see all three words fulfilled—in heaven's timing and in heaven's way.

We must be faithful to the Lord on a daily basis and allow his promises to happen, instead of forcing heavenly provision with earthly means. It won't work because He will not share his glory. No flesh will be able to boast on that final day. God initiated it, God promised it, God made provision for it!

To one He says, "Sell your home and come follow Me," though it may not be convenient in earth's timing. He says, "Now is the time to get out of this business. Now is the time to go to school."

Everyone around you is saying, "What in the world are you doing with your life? You're going to starve."

But our lives must be subject to heaven's timing. Earth's

timing is fine as long as it doesn't conflict with heaven's, and when there is a conflict we must be sensitive enough and confident enough to move according to heaven.

The voice and witness in your spirit crying out that it is heaven's timing to act must be louder than the voice of the world telling you it's not!

An Angel's Perspective

After he explained how they don't understand our faith walk, I asked my angel, "What was it like when Lucifer fell?"

He thought for a moment, like he was trying to choose his words carefully so I would understand, and said,

"It was a battle between the angels. If you can understand this, for the most part, God stayed out of it."

I asked, "What do you mean?" And he quoted me Revelation 12, verses 7 and 8:

"And there was war in heaven, and <u>Michael and his angels</u> fought against the dragon; and <u>the dragon fought and his angels</u>."

He went into some detail talking about how there was a dividing up of sides and Michael was the one who rallied the angels for God. He said Michael took the initiative to oppose Lucifer and organized the angels. He also said Michael spoke against Lucifer to the other angels and exposed Lucifer's deceit to the rest of them.

"Michael was the chief one who rallied the angels."

After the war the Lord rearranged assignments and reward and promotion were given accordingly. In Jude 9 Michael is called the archangel and in Daniel 12:1 he is named as the one who is in charge of defending Israel.

The Bible says in Revelation 12:8 that there was **"found no place"** for the dragon and he was cast out.

In Matthew 25:41 Jesus said that hell was **"prepared for the devil and his angels."**

There was found no place for them. At the time of this war there was just God and the angels. Nothing but love, joy, peace—only the attributes of God filling the universe. Lucifer rejected God and all that is part of His presence and led a third of the angels in rebellion. There was found no place for them.

Where in the universe could the Lord put those who had rejected all that is God? Where could they go to get away from all that love and joy and peace they had just rejected?

God in His mercy prepared a place where His presence wasn't manifested and that place is called hell. It is a place where God's presence isn't manifested because Lucifer rejected the Lord. It was originally prepared according to Matthew 25:41, as a place for satan and his angels, and not intended to be for people.

God planned for people to be with him in heaven.

I looked at this angel and realized suddenly that he was very, very old, and so I asked him, "How old are you?" He looked at me with all seriousness and he said:

"Billions. And remember, I saw the earth created."

This is recorded in Job 38:7:

"...and all the sons of God shouted for joy."

Angels have been around a very long time. They move at the command of the Lord. They know what it is to fight for what is right and they have made the right choice! They are wholly committed to obeying the Lord, and a large part of that obedience is preparing things for you and I! We must move with heaven's timing and what we sense in our spirits, while walking wisely in this natural world.

Angels Fix a Car

Some friends of ours are missionaries in the country of Panama. They minister to the Choco Indians who live in the Darien jungle—some of the thickest jungle in the world.

One day Jeanne and two of her boys were heading down the Pan-American highway towards their home in the jungle when there was an explosion under the hood of their Toyota Land Cruiser. They coasted to a stop about 2½ hours from home and about 5 hours from Panama City!

As they lifted the hood they saw what had happened: the battery had exploded and sent battery acid all over the underside of the hood with twisted wires and shrapnel all over. There was no way they could get it going in that condition. Jeanne told her sons, "You'd better pray hard for this one boys!"

As they sat in their 4x4 and prayed, a new four-door Oldsmobile or Cadillac style vehicle pulled up and five young men in business suits got out. They seemed very out of place on this 4-wheel drive road leading to nowhere with business suits and a new luxury vehicle! They asked in perfect English (in this Spanish speaking country) if she would let them take a look, which she did, although she told them what had happened. The leader just responded:

"Let us take a look at it and see what we can do."

The five of them spread out around the engine compartment and peered under the upraised hood as Jeanne and the boys were asked to sit in their seats.

After just a couple of minutes the main speaker shut the hood and asked Jeanne to turn the key. It started right up to Jeanne's surprise and as she thanked them they got into their car and drove away—continuing in the same direction as she was. After spending a few moments in praise and thanksgiving to the Lord, Jeanne drove the 2½ hours to their home.

Her husband, Dennis, was working out in the front along the road and when she pulled in. She asked him if he had seen anyone in a nice Olds or Cadillac come by. The Pan-American highway comes to a dead end in the jungle shortly after their house and there are no side roads.

In fact, the Pan-Am highway runs from Alaska to the tip of South America unbroken, except for the stretch of impenetrable jungle between Panama and Columbia in the Darien—exactly where their house is located!

Dennis assured her he had been working outside all

day and there had hardly been any vehicle, and certainly not a big luxury car. He asked her to pull on in and he'd take a look under the hood.

When she turned off the engine and they lifted the hood they found it in exactly the condition as Jeanne had seen it after the explosion! There was no battery, few wires were left intact and pieces of plastic and lead were all over. She had started the vehicle and driven 2½ hours with no battery and no wires to connect anything!

It later cost them over $2,000 to have their Toyota hauled to Panama City and repaired. Angels and God's provision are there for us when we move in heaven's timing!

Missed the Timing, God Makes it Up!

There is also good news in the scripture for those who have missed heaven's timing in their lives. Three gospels record Jesus walking on the water: **Matthew 14:22-33**; **Mark 6:45-52**; and **John 6:15-21**. Each account provides a slightly different perspective of the same event.

All three record that Jesus told the disciples to go to the other side of the lake while he sent the people away and then went up into the mountains to pray. Mark 6:48 tells us that when Jesus was walking on the water, he **"would have passed by them"** in the boat. It wasn't until they cried out for fear that Jesus altered his course and, as Matthew records, extended an invitation to Peter to walk on the water.

Jesus would have walked right on by them. Why? Because Jesus had given them an order. His order was for them to go to the other side of the lake. Yes it was windy that night, but the order stood, and he was going to hold to his plan to be at the other side by morning.

Jesus is the same today as he was then. He issues orders for our lives and expects to meet us on the other side. Yes, he knows the contrary winds make it difficult, but he expects us to be there! The good news is that he is merciful.

You might be thinking, "John, you said there was good news for those of us who have missed heaven's timing, where is it?" The answer is found in John's recording of this event. John 6:21 says:

"Then they willingly received him into the ship: and <u>immediately the ship was at the land whither they went.</u>"

They had been delayed by the wind and waves, and all their rowing had gotten them only part-way across the lake. Jesus wanted to walk on by them to keep his divine appointment on the other side. But when they cried out with fear Jesus came over to them, and, after Peter walked, sank, then walked back to the boat with Jesus.

Jesus stepped into the boat **"and immediately the ship was at the land whither they went."**

Jesus transported a whole boat with twelve men plus himself to the other side of the lake so he could keep with heaven's timing!

Perhaps you, too, started on a journey you knew the Lord had commanded, but the contrary winds of circumstance and human frailty kept you rowing hard against them, not making progress, though in your heart you wanted to be with

Jesus on the other side.

Good news! When Jesus gets into your boat he will make up for lost time by transporting you to where you should have been all along—with nothing lost! Cry out to him and allow him to come to the boat of your life. He will restore you back into heaven's plan and set your life to be in unison with heaven's timing.

3

The Fullness of the Time

"But when the <u>fullness of the time</u> was come, God sent forth his Son, made of a woman, made under the law." Galatians 4:4

As my angel stood there talking to me about heaven I asked him:

"How do you relate to Jesus?"

In my mind I realized they had seen everything Jesus had done for man. He started talking about Jesus being worthy to be worshiped and glorified; he said:

"You have to understand, we know Him as Creator."

Then, slower to let me grasp what he was saying:

"We know Him as Creator. He is worthy to be glorified and you are worthy to serve over us because He loves you so very much."

He continued, "Though we knew what was taking place when he left heaven, we did not personally understand. We had no way of comparing his great act of love for you with anything we had ever experienced or had ever seen him do."

"The creation of the universe pales beside the act of Him leaving heaven to become one of his creations."

When Jesus Left Heaven

And with those words I was instantly in the Spirit.

I believe I was given a glimpse of the moment in time when Jesus left heaven to be conceived in Mary and enter the earth. I saw a long corridor formed by angels on either side from the front of the throne of the Father. I saw many, many angels along the sides, like so many thousands of people at a huge parade all crowded along the parade route, though in perfect unity and order. They were in silence as they were bowing from the waist.

Every single angel realized the gravity of what was about to happen.

The Creator was about to leave his home and become one of his creations. His relationship with his Father was about to change forever. There was no sense of depression or sadness, just an overwhelming sense of the seriousness of what was being done.

Even the multi-winged cherubs at each corner of the throne platform had their wings and heads bowed in silence. Out of this intense light where the throne was, Jesus stepped out of the light of his Father and walked steadily away and passed through the path between the angels.

No one said a word. He never looked back. It was at

that moment He left heaven.

Hebrews 10:5-7 records the final conversation between the Father and his Son:

"Wherefore when he cometh [AMP *entered*] **into the world, he saith, 'Sacrifice and offering thou wouldest not, but a body hast thou prepared me:**
In burnt offerings and sacrifices for sin thou hast had no pleasure.
Then said I, Lo, I come (in the volume of the book it is written of me)—speaking of the Old Testament—**to do thy will, O God.'"**

Notice, **"but a body thou hast prepared me."** This is talking about being conceived within Mary and taking on him human flesh. Philippians 2:7,8:

"...and took upon him the form of a servant, and was made in the likeness of men: And being found in fashion as a man..."

Our Lord had eternal pre-existence with the Father, but he didn't stay in the Spirit. He left heaven to take upon him the flesh of his creation that he might die for our salvation.

My angel continued, "We do not comprehend His great love for you, that He would strip Himself of all authority and honor and lay it down and would become one of His creation. That He would give all that up for man. We do not understand this."

Galatians 4:4 **"But when the fullness of the time was come, God sent forth his Son..."**

From heaven's perspective, when the Father said it was time for Jesus to leave heaven and be clothed with human flesh, it was time.

Jesus, born in Bethlehem under a wicked ruler that would try to kill him, was within the "fullness of the time." Having Mary and Joseph travel to Bethlehem only to find no room in the inn was in the "fullness of the time."

Heaven's "fullness of the time" doesn't mean everything is going to be perfect, it means that God, having taken every element into consideration, has deemed the time at hand to be "the fullness of time," and therefore time to act.

The Stage is Set

Fullness means it can't hold any more. It means everything is set and it couldn't be any more ready for heaven's event to come to pass.

Whether that's a move across the country, a job change, or any other action we take when we sense heaven's timing and the fullness of the time in our lives, God has made provision.

Think about what had to happen in the natural and political realm on this earth before Galatians 4:4 records that it was **"the fullness of the time"** to send Jesus to us.

There was a silent time between the book of Malachi and Matthew of about 400 years, 400 silent years. In the meantime, the Persian Empire fell, and the Greeks were raised up. Alexander the Great of Greece gave the Mediterranean world a common language, which would facilitate the writing of the gospel. (Our New Testament is written for the most part in Greek.) He provided roads. He instituted Hellenism, the Greek culture, all over the Mediterranean world. Then the Romans came in and borrowed from the Greeks. They made the roads better. They conquered the whole area. Transportation, central government, and a court system were all established.

All these events later helped facilitate the spreading of the gospel, and it was in that time that God deemed to be 'the fullness.' All the different elements were in place so that He could act to send his son.

Even though you may think you're ready to move on a direction from God, the other elements around you may not have yet been prepared. It is not the fullness of the time. Be patient. God so loved the world that He gave His Son but He didn't blow it by sending Him early. He sent Him when the fullness of the time was set.

Most of the time when the Lord speaks to us it comes first in the little perceptions, in the little intuitions, in the little hunches we have. We might say: "I feel like it's just stirring around in me. I feel like a change is coming." Or, "I just feel like I'm supposed to go to school." Or, "I think I'm supposed to go to this city or this job." Or, "It's just stirring around in me that I've got to do this or I've got to do that."

We're trained in the world to react to *our* circumstances only and to make sure they are in place before we move, and yet the Lord didn't wait until every little thing was in order.

The Father sent forth his Son because he deemed it was the fullness of the time, based on his knowledge. That didn't mean he was sending his son into a perfect world where everyone would immediately perceive who Jesus was and receive him.

Sometimes we want everything to be perfect before we convince ourselves something is God.

That's really just an excuse to give in to our fears and satan uses it to keep us out of the fullness of what the Lord has for us. All the elements and circumstances aren't always going to line up, but *we have to make priority decisions from our spirit man based on our eternal destiny, not on what the circumstances say.*

Circumstances will never lead you into your eternal destiny.

We must move with heaven's timing. Like Peter did when he left the fishing business, like Matthew did when he left his job as a tax collector, and like Noah did when he started building an ark when there wasn't a cloud in the sky. Noah prepared the ark for many years, but the rain didn't come **"until the fullness of the time."** Don't try to float until your ark is prepared, but build when heaven says, "build." It has well been said:

"The evidence of the call is the willingness to prepare."

The Fullness of the Time in My Life

My wife and I were high school sweethearts who, after graduating from high school, entered into the same university our parents had attended. It was the thing to do. I was a year ahead in school so I was a sophomore when she was a freshman.

We each knew we would be married and enter into the ministry, and we also knew this secular school was not in God's plans for our ministerial training. We went in obedience to our parents, and also from a sense that we really didn't have any clear direction from the Lord yet.

In September of the first semester of my sophomore year (the first semester of Barb's freshman year) Barb and I were praying and the Lord told me we could be married in September of the next year. He also said that my dad would cut off the money for college at the Christmas break. He didn't tell me what to do after that.

Imagine my thoughts when the Lord told me on the one hand we could be married next year, and then saying that I wouldn't be back to school! He didn't share what he had in mind at that time.

I had to walk by the peace he had given me and wait for the fullness of the time.

I went through the motions from September through mid-December, not knowing what waited for me in the new year.

When I met with my dad during Christmas break it was decided that if I wanted to go back to school it would be by my own funds. My immaturity had kept me from really applying myself during my first two years so my grades were barely above average, but I really didn't want to be there.

The Lord told me over the holidays to spend some time fasting, praying, and waiting on him. At a New Year's Eve service a girl came up to me a little nervous. She said, "John, during praise and worship the Lord gave me a scripture for you. I hope it makes sense. It's Psalm 27:13-14."

"I had fainted, unless I had believed to see the goodness of the Lord in the land of the living. Wait on the Lord: be of good courage and he shall strengthen thine heart: wait I say, on the Lord."

I went home and spent the next three months "waiting on the Lord." I was a healthy 19-year-old living at home, the oldest of four children with a single mom. I couldn't get a release to get a job, and yet the time for me to propose to Barb was quickly approaching. My mom went to the Lord on two occasions about this and both times the Lord told her it was from him that I was doing this. I was so zealous to follow the Lord my mom did ask me once, "Did the Lord tell you not to empty the trash or help around the house?" I came back to center after that and realized I didn't have to disassociate myself from my family. Thank you, mom!

Preview of Ministry to Come

The Lord seemed to especially teach me about prayer and healing during this time. In March, I proposed to Barb and we set a date in September to be married. I had no job, no car, no plans, and I was a happy, healthy 19-year-old! On Easter night, I was at a service with our group of teens at a friend's house when the leader had a word of knowledge, "There is someone here who the Lord has been teaching about healing." There were only about 12 of us in the group and nobody raised their hands.

Finally, realizing it was me, I raised my hand. He

called me out and then asked if there was someone who needed healing. A girl with scoliosis stepped forward. Her left shoulder was at least 1-inch lower than her right shoulder and her whole manner of carrying herself was off-center.

Dave, the leader of our group and now a pastor in Kentucky, said, "John, there you go." I asked him what he wanted me to do, and he said just do what the Lord has been teaching me. I really didn't know what to do, so I asked her to step forward and lightly ran my hand from the small of her back up to her neck as I said, "In the name of Jesus, be healed."

Suddenly she started shaking from the base of her spine up. The shaking started low and seemed to move up her spine like a terrier shaking a snake. It only took about 15 seconds, but when the shaking moved to her upper back her shoulder straightened up and became normal! I touched her lightly on the forehead and she fell out under the power of God.

For the next two weeks, it seemed that anyone who needed healing got healed when I laid hands on him or her. My mom had bruised her thigh and as she sat on the sofa one night she said:

"If the Lord has given you this power to heal, then heal my leg."

We stepped into the living room and she stood in front of the sofa as I touched her leg and then her forehead "in the name of Jesus." She fell backwards onto the sofa and got up healed. Our neighbor across the street had run his elbow through a hollow door and it was very stiff and sore. The same thing happened to him.

Moving by Revelation

At the end of the two weeks it seemed the anointing lifted. I later asked the Lord why he did that and he replied, "I just wanted to show you what you're going to be doing later." Two weeks to the night Dave had another word for me. "The Lord is telling me to tell you to obey your mother, because she is going to have a word for you."

On Tuesday afternoon mom walked through the door and said, "The Lord told me you are supposed to fly to Tulsa." I thought she was kidding, but she went straight for the phone and made the reservation. I left town the next morning with $9 and my mom's VISA card.

I didn't know anything about Tulsa or why I was there. I toured Oral Roberts University and even applied for a job, but the hand of the Lord was so strong on me I couldn't finish the application. The lady told me to sign it and they'd keep it on file anyway. Later that day, I went to Rhema Bible Training Center in Broken Arrow, a suburb of Tulsa. I didn't feel particularly led there either.

That night, now down to seven dollars and going nowhere fast, I sought the Lord. As I was kneeling in prayer I saw in the Spirit a river being held back by two gates. On the water, like letters floating on alphabet cereal, I saw "Charlotte." The gates opened and the word floated on down stream.

I called my mom and told her the Lord told me to go to Charlotte and asked her what was there. She said, "The PTL Club is there. It's OK because Betty (our neighbor across the street) was vacuuming her house today at about four o'clock and suddenly Jesus appeared right in front of her vacuum and said, 'I'm going to send John to work for the PTL Club.' Then he disappeared. So go ahead and charge the airline ticket."

When I walked into the employment office at PTL I learned there was a hiring freeze. As I told my story to the lady behind the desk she looked as disinterested as someone who had heard it 100 times before. I completed the application but didn't know what position to apply for. I took it back to her and she said, "Go pray about it." I sat back down and prayed for a couple of minutes before I heard the Lord say, "Put down 'Tour Guide.'"

When I walked over to the desk, the lady was looking at me kind of funny. She said, "When you were over there praying, the Lord told me to hire you." Through a series of interviews it was decided I would be hired for work at Heritage USA. I transferred to be under the Park Ranger department and began work in early May. It was the fullness of the time that I wait for my mom to get a word! Now I had a job in another state with a Christian ministry! I was elated.

Now I had a job, but still no car. I was getting rides from co-workers to and from work and walking to the store, laundry, etc. One day in August, just a month before the wedding, the Lord was teaching me about marriage. He was just finishing talking to me about how I should lay down my life for my wife and treat her like a queen. Then he said, "By the way, the reason I sent you to Tulsa is because I want you to go to Rhema next fall." He also told me to put legs to my faith and go buy a car because one had been provided. I was to stop limiting him to one way of getting me a car: I had been looking for someone to give me one.

I picked up the phone to call my mom and tell her I

was supposed to go to Rhema next fall, and she happened to be having lunch with a friend. Unknown to us, this friend had been told by the Lord in March:

"In about a year and a half I'm going to send John to Rhema, and I want you to pay his tuition."

She held onto that word; now it was August and she and my mom just happened to be having lunch together. She said, "Mail me a copy of your acceptance letter and I'll write the check." I did, and she did! Later that day I went to a Chrysler dealership and bought a new car with no money down! Now I had a car and a job, with the wedding only a month away.

For six months I hadn't known why I had flown to Tulsa, but the Lord told me when it was his time. I held onto the peace I had in my spirit even though my head was screaming for answers, but heaven's timing is always best! The fullness of the time by heaven's figuring isn't always the same as man's way of thinking. How many people would figure on quitting college, spend three months in prayer and fasting, fly half way across the country first one way and then another, to have someone in the midst of a hiring freeze tell you God told them to hire you!

If we allow the Lord to do things in his timing we won't always be understood by others, but when you have his timing in your spirit you won't lack anything.

4

Discerning the Timing

Moving in heaven's timing means being willing to submit our daily agendas to subtle influences in our spirit, as we've trained our senses to discern these leadings in the spirit man.

One day our family was planning to go to the Cheyenne Mountain Zoo in Colorado Springs, Colorado. We lived about 1½ hours from there and we needed to get out of town and away for awhile, but I always pray about our plans. In my mind I play out the day as I pray. I had a 'check' in my spirit about part of the trip, but I didn't have clarity on what part.

As I prayed I went through the day in my mind. I thought about us loading up in our Suburban and heading down the two-lane highway heading west. As I prayed in the Spirit my mind was both thinking about the trip and also focused on my spirit man. I thought, "What is this 'check' I sense? Is it the truck?" I prayed a little bit about the truck and the mechanics of the trip, thinking about the hot day, spare tire, enough coolant in the radiator and the like, but I had a peace in my spirit about that aspect. Still, unrest persisted in another area, only I didn't know which one.

As I prayed I turned my attention to my wife Barb and our three boys, Chris, Jason, and Brian. As I prayed about the boys the 'check', or heavy feeling I had, grew stronger.

I quickly scanned Brian and Jason in my mind—meaning I thought quickly about them—and had a peace. The heavy feeling lifted when I thought about them. When I thought about Chris the heaviness in my spirit told my mind that I had zeroed in on the issue the Father wanted me to see.

I thought about him walking around the zoo on his walker: Chris has cerebral palsy, and at that time walked with a walker due to weakness in his legs. (Cerebral palsy is defined as an injury to the brain sustained during labor or delivery, in his case, lack of oxygen.)

As I prayed from my spirit and thought with my mind about him at the zoo, I began to have a strong sense of something related to weather hurting or killing him. As I continued to pray I sensed a lightning strike from a thunderstorm. After taking authority over that evil plan to kill my son and getting a peace about continuing the trip, I prepared the family to go.

We went to the zoo and had a wonderful time for the first hour or so. While we were in one of the buildings I lost track of Chris. Unknown to us, a thunderstorm had moved quickly over the mountains, and the next thing I knew we heard thunder. I ran outside as it started pouring rain and found Chris speeding along on his wheeled walker having a great time and getting soaked! I grabbed him under my arm and ran for the shelter of the building, and had only been inside for about 45 seconds when a lightning bolt hit near where Chris had been. He most certainly would have been injured or killed had I not been on the lookout! We finished the zoo and had a wonderful time that afternoon.

The key was that I sensed something in my spirit, then took the time to pray it through until I had eliminated what it wasn't, and determined what the Father was speaking into my life.

Every major decision I make is made this way, and many minor ones. Often when I don't know the direction to go in my mind I think of the two or three possibilities as I pray. I think about what I would do if I chose path #1—do I have a peace in my spirit while I think about going in this direction? Then I pray and simultaneously think about direction #2—do I have a peace about going in this direction?

After disciplining the mind to **"by reason of use"** discern **"between good and evil,"** the direction that bears witness in my spirit by peace becomes apparent. The other options feel like a "hold," or "check," or heaviness in my spirit, so no matter what my mind says about how wonderful it would be to go that way, I overrule my mind with the peace in my spirit.

Jesus received direction and made decisions in much the same way. In John 11 we read the story of Lazarus being raised from the dead. Note verses 3-10:

"Therefore his sisters sent unto him saying, Lord, behold, he whom thou lovest is sick.
When Jesus heard that, he said, 'This sickness is not unto death, but for the glory of God, that the Son of God might be glorified thereby:'
Now Jesus loved Martha, and her sister, and Lazarus.
When he had heard therefore that he was sick, he abode two days still in the same place where he was.
Then after that saith he to his disciples, Let us go into Judea again.

His disciples say unto him, Master, the Jews of late sought to stone thee; and goest thou thither again?

Jesus answered, 'Are there not twelve hours in the day? <u>If any man walk in the day</u>, he stumbleth not, <u>because he seeth the light of this world.</u>

But if a man walk in the night, he stumbleth, because there is no light in him.'"

In the previous two chapters in the gospel of John we read that Jesus was nearly stoned, and there was plotting and an effort in 10:39 to capture him, but he escaped to the place beyond the Jordan river where John first began his ministry. It was there that Jesus heard that his friend Lazarus was sick.

When Jesus first heard the natural news of the illness in verse 3: **"Lord, behold, he whom thou lovest is sick,"** Jesus responded with the spiritual news his Father revealed to him in verse 4:

"This sickness is not unto [will not end up with] **death, but for the glory of God, that the Son of God may be glorified thereby."**

Jesus received natural information, but he received and believed the supernatural information from the Spirit of God more. Receiving the spiritual information along with the natural information is crucial to moving in heaven's timing. Both areas of knowledge must come together in their proper timing before we move.

Verse 6 tells us that when he heard Lazarus was sick and he knew the end result wouldn't be death he stayed two days longer where he was in hiding. Once Jesus received word

Discerning the Timing 85

from above that the sickness wouldn't end in death, it didn't matter whether he stayed two days or two weeks because he knew the outcome. The only thing left was the timing of when Lazarus' healing would be manifest and God glorified!

Verse 7 tells us that after the two days Jesus said in effect, "Now it's time for us to go to Judea again." The disciples in verse eight raised the point that they were where they were because they nearly got stoned, so why would Jesus go back into Judea? In fact, verse 16 records that Thomas, upon seeing the determination of Jesus to return declared, **"Let us also go, that we may die with him."**

The situation was that they escaped for their lives beyond Jordan where Jesus learned his friend was sick. Jesus had stayed in hiding because he was nearly captured, and he had received revelation from above that the sickness wouldn't end in death anyway, so it was just a matter of getting the "all clear" from the Father on when to go see Lazarus.

It is in Jesus' response to the question, "Why do you want to go back there since they wanted to stone you?" that he shows us how to move with heaven's timing. He asks:

"Are there not 12 hours in the day? If any man walk in the day, he stumbleth not, because he seeth the light of this world."

Jesus uses the natural sunlight as an example of moving in God's timing and revelation. To all natural appearances, it was suicide to go back to Judea again, but according to heaven's timing it was safe to return. Jesus certainly had to deal with the emotions of his love for Lazarus, the expectations his sisters placed on him, and the lack of understanding of the disciples.

The light he was walking by indicated that even though the natural circumstances appeared unchanged, it was now safe to return.

The fullness of heaven's timing is not always convenient, but then, the natural man cannot receive from the Spirit of God anyway, so one should get used to moving according to spiritual knowledge. The result in this case was that Jesus returned safely, Lazarus was raised from the dead, and many believed in Jesus because of it.

Jesus stated in verse 15 that he was glad he didn't go back when Lazarus was only sick "to the intent ye may believe." If we stay in heaven's timing God is glorified and faith in the Lord is produced.

We were not around at creation to see the earth created like the angels, and yet we're willing to rearrange our lives and do things for the Lord. But are you willing to move according to heaven's timing and wait until the fullness of time has come to fulfill God's destiny? Are you willing to get involved in the different aspects of church, or helping someone in a grocery store, just feeling a prompting in your spirit to go speak to someone?

Angels cannot comprehend how you and I will restructure our lives or make decisions based on leadings from the Holy Spirit. They are sent to prepare the way for us to walk according to heaven's timing. According to heaven's **fullness of time.**

Purpose now to move according to the fullness of heaven's timing. This may be as simple as a nudge in your spirit to get out of bed some night and spend time in prayer. It may be as complex as moving half way around the world to go to the mission field in some distant land. Both require your mind to notice the witness in your spirit enough to get your attention and then take action. According to Hebrews 5:14, the **"strong meat"** of life in God is for those who do indeed train their senses, through reason of use, to discern good and evil.

The Witness Versus the Lord Said

Part of discerning and perceiving the things of God is realizing who or what is speaking. Many Christians walk around saying, "the Lord told me," when in fact they may have just felt a leading in their spirit. Other times people say: "It could have been an audible voice it was so loud when the Lord spoke to me." The trouble is that most people don't know the difference between their spirit, a witness in the spirit, and the Holy Spirit.

Notice what the scripture says about the Holy Spirit speaking to people.

Acts 8:29 **"Then the Spirit said unto Philip, Go near, and join thyself to this chariot."**

Acts 10:19 **"While Peter thought on the vision, the Spirit said unto him, Behold, three men seek thee."**

Acts 13:2 **"As they ministered to the Lord and fasted, the Holy Ghost said, Separate me Barnabus and Saul for the work whereunto I have called them."**

Acts 21:11 **"Thus saith the Holy Ghost, So shall**

the Jews at Jerusalem bind the man that owneth this girdle, and shall deliver him into the hands of the Gentiles."

Notice that in each instance when the Holy Spirit speaks, the directions are very clear and precise. Usually when some dear brother or sister talks about the Lord talking to them and says, "His voice was so loud it could have been audible," they experienced the Holy Spirit speaking to them. In each of the testimonies I've heard along these lines, the person received very specific direction from the Lord.

As we can see from Acts 21, a prophecy can be delivered in this manner. Usually, prophecy will not be as clear. According to I Corinthians 14:3 the gift of prophecy manifests for the purpose of edification, exhortation, and comfort. There have been times I have heard the Holy Spirit speak very clearly to me about a word of knowledge or something prophetic in nature, but most of the time the word begins forming in my spirit rather than the Holy Spirit himself talking to me.

Let's look at the way angels speak to people:

Acts 8:26 **"And the angel of the Lord spake unto Philip, saying, Arise, and go toward the south unto the way that goeth down from Jerusalem unto Gaza, which is desert."**

Acts 10:3-6 **"...an angel of God coming in to him, and saying unto him, Cornelius...Thy prayers are come up for a memorial before God. And now send men to Joppa, and call for one Simon, whose surname is Peter: He lodgeth with one Simon..."**

Acts 12:7 **"And, behold, the angel of the Lord
came upon him, and a light shined in the prison:
and he smote Peter on the side, and raised him up,
saying, Arise up quickly. And his chains fell off from
his hands."**

Notice that when angels speak they are very specific
and precise in their directions as well. There is no vagueness
or ambiguity with either the Holy Spirit speaking or an angel.
They do have different and distinct voices. In Acts 8:26 an
angel speaks to Philip to head off down the road to the desert,
and in verse 29 it is the Holy Spirit that speaks to him to
join the chariot of the Ethiopian eunuch. Both instructions
were very clear, yet distinct from each other. In each case,
these words were not vague feelings or "a witness" that left
questions in their minds.

Now let's look at what happens when people receive a
witness from the Holy Spirit into the spirit man. We will see
that when the Holy Spirit speaks into our spirit and it has
to be noticed, then discerned and perceived by the mind of
the person, the result is vagueness and a certain uncertainty.
Acts 20:22-23:

**"And now, behold, I go bound in the spirit
unto Jerusalem, <u>not knowing the things that shall
befall me</u> there: Save that the <u>Holy Ghost witnesses</u>
in every city, saying that bonds and affliction abide
me."**

Paul said that he didn't know what was going to
happen to him except that the Holy Spirit "witnesses" in
every city that bonds and affliction await him. He didn't have
the details from the Holy Spirit, just the "witness" that bonds

and affliction awaited him.

We get an idea how the Holy Spirit witnessed to him by looking at the reaction of the people in Acts 21:4: **"…who said to Paul through the Spirit, that he should not go up to Jerusalem."** Notice that there is no, "the Holy Spirit said" in this passage. One translator puts it this way: "…who said to Paul through impressions made by the Spirit." They had the same witness he had been given, but they didn't have the specific details.

It wasn't until Paul enters into Philip's house that the prophet Agabus comes to him and gives him the specifics about the witness he had been receiving. Verse 11:

"Thus saith the Holy Ghost, So shall the Jews at Jerusalem bind the man that owneth this girdle, and shall deliver him into the hands of the Gentiles."

Up until that point all Paul knew was that the Holy Spirit <u>witnessed</u> that "bonds and affliction await me." When Agabus shared what the Holy Spirit <u>said</u>, he learned it would be the Jews who would arrest him and they in turn would turn him over to the Romans (Gentiles). This is new information and again, very specific.

In Acts 27 Paul has been arrested as the Holy Spirit had said through Agabus and now he is on a ship destined for Rome. In verse 10 Paul says:

"Sirs, I perceive that this voyage will be with hurt and much damage, not only of the lading and ship, but also of our lives."

Notice that Paul said he "perceived." He didn't say,

"the Lord told me." This is the error many Christians get into when they perceive something in their spirit and then add on 'the Lord told me.' What did Paul perceive? The voyage would be with hurt and damage to: the cargo, the ship, and their lives. This was something he perceived. It revealed what would happen if things continued upon their present course.

Here's the point: What Paul perceived was partly wrong!

The ship and cargo were lost, but nobody died. Many times the Lord gives us a witness or we perceive events in our spirits that which will occur if nothing changes. In other words, the Lord will often use 'perception' as a means of revealing satan's plans which will occur unless God intervenes.

Many Christians have run around trying to rebuke what the Holy Spirit has put in their spirit when they perceived something bad about to happen. Instead of recognizing what they perceived as being in the spirit, they rebuked it!

After a time of fasting (v 21) Paul received a specific word from an angel and tells about it starting in verse 22:

"And now I exhort you to be of good cheer: for <u>there shall be no loss of any man's life</u> among you, but of the ship.

For there stood by me this night the angel of God, whose I am, and whom I serve.

Saying, Fear not, Paul; thou must be brought before Caesar: and, lo, God hath given thee all them that sail with thee."

Verse 26 **"Howbeit we must be cast upon a certain island."**

Verse 3: **"Except these abide in the ship ye cannot be saved."**

Before, all Paul had was a perception in his spirit that the cargo, ship, and their lives would be lost. Now, with a specific word from the angel he learns that he will go before Caesar, nobody will die, they will be shipwrecked, and later in verse 31 that everyone had to stay with the ship until it ran aground for them to be safe. That's specific!

If you think back over your Christian life, there may have been times you heard the Lord "from the outside." It would have been a very specific direction or warning. That was either the Holy Spirit or an angel. An angel's voice carries the presence of the Lord, but with a lesser anointing that is similar in feel—in the spirit—to a person speaking with anointing. The Holy Spirit, on the other hand, can also be from the outside, but stronger in tone and anointing and spoken with the authority of God and 'feel' in the spirit. Something perceived or discerned in our spirit man is internal and as we have seen, more vague.

Something we perceive or discern about an event in the future may be subject to intervention from God. One night as I was drifting off to sleep I had an uneasy witness in my spirit about one of the students at the university we had ministered to. As I prayed what I perceived became clearer until I heard the Holy Spirit say, "Satan has a contract on Laurie's life tonight and you need to stop it." Along with his voice came a vision of Laurie riding in a car with her friend Jackie driving. They pulled onto the highway and were nearly run off the road and killed by a reckless car that sideswiped them and made their car roll down a hill.

As I saw this I said, "Satan, I forbid you from taking

Laurie's life tonight and command your plans to be broken in the name of Jesus. Father, please send your angels to protect them. Amen."

About ten days later I saw Laurie at a service and asked her if she had been in town the previous week. Before I had a chance to bring up that specific event, she told me they had, and then excitedly told me that they had nearly been killed that night by a car trying to run them off the road, but Jackie saw it at the last moment and swerved out of his way. The accident never happened because God intervened. Paul's life and the lives aboard his ship weren't lost because God intervened. Both cases started off revealing the plan of satan if left unchecked.

What began as something perceived in my spirit became the specific voice of the Holy Spirit giving me a warning for a friend. Thank the Lord I knew the difference and didn't try to rebuke the Holy Spirit!

5

Seasons

"To every thing there is a season, and a time to every purpose under the heaven." Ecclesiastes 3:1

Notice that there is a season and there is a purpose for every season. In the Greek language there are two main words that are used to identify what we call "time." One means a duration, a long time. It's the word in the Greek language "**chronos**." It's where we get "chronological order." For example, your watch is a chronometer.

The second word is "**kairos**." This word means, "season." A season identifies a quality of time. We may think of a year going by and think of chronos, but spring, summer, winter and fall are seasons, or "kairos."

There are, in fact, seasons to our lives. There are times when you may have been in a job and you know going in, "This is a job for now, but I just have an idea that I'm not going to be here that long." Or maybe you take in a boarder, or you take in a child, or you help a family member out. You know going into it that it's temporary. Maybe you take care of an elderly loved one, or you go and visit such and such a person or a place, or you enter into a particular ministry, or you get involved with something and you say inside, "I know that God is having me do this now, but it's just for a season." It's for a time. And that's what we're talking about.

Ecclesiastes 3:1: **"To every thing there is a purpose, there is a season and a time to every purpose under heaven."**

Notice some of the things that Ecclesiastes lists:

"A time to be born, and a time to die; a time to plant, and a time to pluck up that which is planted;

A time to kill, a time to heal; a time to break down, a time to build up;

A time to weep, a time to laugh; a time to mourn, a time to dance;

A time to cast away stones, and a time to gather stones together; [That's talking about tearing down something built and then gathering materials to build up anew.]

A time to embrace, and a time to refrain from embracing;

A time to get, and a time to lose; a time to keep, and a time to cast away;

A time to rend, and a time to sew; a time to keep silence, and a time to speak;

A time to love, and a time to hate; a time of war, and a time of peace."

What profit has he that works in that wherein he labours?"

Verses 1-8 identify several different seasons in our lives. And verse 9 says:

"What profit has he that works in that wherein he works?"

In other words, what profit is there for you in your

work? You go through all these times and all these seasons and we say, "Well, what profit is there of working in this season?" Or, "What good did that experience do me?"

Verse 10 says: **"I have seen the travail, which God has given to the sons of men to be exercised** [trained] **in it."**

One of the purposes for seasons and for working in that season is that it's training for you and I. It is personal enrichment time. It is personal discipleship time. It's character development time. In each season there is an aspect of training.

Have you ever found a job that you know is from God, but that it's for a season and immediately there are challenges with people or systems, and you think, "What is the purpose?" Well, the purpose is: how will you handle yourself in the midst of that season? How will we handle ourselves when there are difficulties? The Lord is watching us to see if we will mature within the season he gives us. Will we discover his reason for the season and learn? Will we be aware that we are there according to heaven's timing and in heaven's fullness, and just because all the elements aren't perfect doesn't mean it isn't God?

Verse 11 says: **"He has made every thing beautiful in his time...."**

Every season has a time of beauty if we will be faithful to endure and work and do what we need to do within that season. Notice, **"he has made everything beautiful <u>in his time.</u>"** The beauty doesn't reveal itself at the beginning.

The beauty of a season is manifest in the maturity of

the season.

Spring starts out cold and brown, but the beauty is revealed towards the end—towards summer—with splashes of flowers and new growth. Summer starts out with flowers and trees, but the beauty of summer is in the lush fullness of mature growth. The beauty of fall is in the changing colors, and we think of the beauty of winter being revealed in delicate formations of snow flakes and icicles. Be assured that every season will reveal its beauty "in its time."

Galatians 6:9 says: **"And let us not be weary in well doing, for in due season we shall reap, if we faint not."** You will reap what you have sown. You will reap that faithfulness and the lesson learned. There is a season of development within you and I. It has a beginning and it has an end. It is work; it is training. It is exercising those gifts that are within us. Verse 11 says that if we will fulfill this, if we'll walk in this, it will be beautiful in its time. It will come to completion.

There are times in those jobs that we know we're there for a season and it seems like just in the last week or last month of that job, it suddenly all comes together, and then about that time, God says, "I want you to go someplace else." Why? Because the season has drawn to a close. He has made it beautiful in its season. The fulfillment has come. You have learned what you needed to learn and off you go to another season.

You have to realize that from heaven's perspective, the whole reason God brought you to that job you've had for the last two years may have been for the last two months when the boss got sick and you were the only one who knew how to run everything. Or it may have been just so you could tell one certain co-worker about Jesus. Of course, the Father's purpose will also always involve character building as well.

In the first chapter of the book of Acts, in verses 6 and 7, Jesus is about ready to ascend up into heaven, and verse 6 says:

"When they came together, they asked of him, saying, Lord, will you at this time restore again the kingdom to Israel?"

In other words, at this time, Jesus, are You going to kick the Romans out of Jerusalem and make Israel the kingdom that it is destined to be? In verse 7 he says:

"It is not for you to know the <u>times</u> or the <u>seasons</u>, which the Father has put in his own power."

Or more literally, **"which the Father has put in His own <u>authority</u>."**

This tells us that it is the Father God Who holds the keys to the seasons in our lives. The Father has hidden the "times" (chronos) and "seasons" (kairos) within his own knowledge. He only lets us know them a little before hand, or he tells us the ultimate destiny and the rest he holds within his own knowledge.

I Corinthians 2:9-10 says:

"Eye has not seen, neither ear heard, neither has entered into the heart of man the things which God has prepared for those that love him. But he has revealed these things to us by his Spirit."

Natural man can't figure out the times and seasons which the Father has kept within himself, but we can learn of them by the Holy Spirit. Jesus said of the Holy Spirit in John 16:13:

"...he will guide you into all truth: for he shall not speak of himself; but whatsoever he shall hear, that shall he speak: and he will show you things to come."

The Holy Spirit speaks to us according to what he hears from the Father and Son. He speaks of the plans, times, and seasons of our lives and guides us into those truths.

You cannot discover the seasons of your life or the purpose in the seasons in your life just by the eyes and the ear, those things are only revealed by the Spirit!

I remember a lady who had a day care service in her home; one day she came to me and said that she could sense on the inside of her that something was going to change, and that it was about three months away, which was the end of the school year. She was sensing that she was no longer going to have the day care in her home—that God was going to move her into something else. She didn't know exactly what. It was just an inner feeling that her involvement with the day care was drawing to a close.

According to the husband of this lady, she was a real grouch to live with the last three months or so that she had this day care in her house. She was agitated and unhappy on the inside and she didn't know why. She just said, "I feel like this is drawing to a close, like God is going to have me do something else, that I'm supposed to shut it down and he's going to give me a job somewhere, but I don't know exactly where that thing is." And she became, in her husband's words, a real bear to live with, because she was agitated and she did not have the answer for that season.

That's the way we are many times when we realize the Father holds the seasons in his own grasp, in his own knowledge, and he's not talking in the way we want him to. It takes the Spirit of God to reveal these things to us in its proper time and in its proper season, but when we don't know, we start asking, "What in the world are you doing with my life?"

In John, chapter 7:1-5 we see that Jesus' family does not yet believe in him:

"After these things Jesus walked in Galilee: for he would not walk in Jewry, because the Jews wanted to kill him. Now the Jews' feast of tabernacles was at hand.

His brethren therefore said to him, Depart hence, and go into Judea, that your disciples may also see the works that thou doest.

For there is no man that doeth any thing in secret, and he himself seeketh to be known openly. If you do these things, show yourself to the world.

For neither did his brethren believe in him."

In other words, they were using sarcasm to their big brother because they did not believe in him. "Jesus, you're doing all these miracles and things that people are talking about. Go on up to the feast of tabernacles and tell everybody about it. Let them see the miracles that you're doing."

Now, technically they were Jesus' half-brothers. These

gentlemen were the product of Mary and Joseph, and at least two of them became believers. (A listing of his brothers is found in Matthew 13:55) One of whom wrote the book of James, and another wrote the book of Jude. So at least these two eventually came around, but at this time they were unbelievers.

Jesus said in verse 6: **"My season,"** and in the Greek, this word is "kairos," or season, a shorter well-defined season of time:

"'My season is not yet come: but your season, is always ready.
The world cannot hate you; but it hates me, because I testify of it, that the works thereof are evil.
Go up to the feast: I don't go up yet to the feast; for <u>my season is not yet *full* come.</u>'
When he had said these words unto them, he stayed in Galilee.
But when his brothers went up to the feast, then he went up also into the feast, not openly, but as it were in secret."

Jesus made a fantastic statement there in verse 6. He said, **"My time** [or my season] **is not yet come, but your season is always."** He said this about the unbelievers, "your season is always."

An unbeliever sets his own seasons.

Unbelievers determine for what purpose and reason they enter into business, or go to school, or get a job. Before you and I were born again and brought into God's family and began being sensitive to the things of the Spirit, we did what we wanted to do when we wanted to do it. If you wanted a vacation, you took a vacation. If you wanted to go someplace for the weekend you went. If you wanted to go fishing, you went fishing. You didn't consult the Father God. Your season, your time, and the seasons of your life were within your own control. You set it. You wanted to go to school, you went to school. You wanted to go to a different place of employment, you did that. Jesus said of His unbelieving brothers, "Your time, your season, is always ready." It is within your own control. And no wonder!

The times and season are hidden within the Father's knowledge, and it takes the Holy Spirit to reveal those things because the natural man can't receive the things of the Spirit of God!

But for himself, Jesus said in verse 6: *"My time [season] is not yet come."* When I was born again and came into the Lord's family, I gave up the right to set my own seasons, just as Jesus did not have the right to set his own seasons. Once a part of the family of God, we submit our plans and season to our Father's will. He alone holds the knowledge of those seasons and their appointed times.

Before I was a believer I did not have the Holy Spirit, so it was always my time (season). My seasons were always within my authority. When we come into the Kingdom of God—and we've been used to setting our own times and seasons—we must submit to the Father's seasons for us, but often it rubs our flesh the wrong way! We don't understand what's trying to be accomplished in these things and why it's better to move according to heaven's timing and sense of completion rather than our own ideas.

Jesus said in verse 8, **"My time** [or my season] **has**

not yet *full* come," but as we read on in verse 10:

"But when his brethren were gone up, then went he also up unto the feast, not openly, but as it were in secret."

He went up and even spoke at the feast. The fullness of the season for him to go to the feast was just a few hours or days off from his unbelieving brothers, but he wasn't going to rush the season. He waited until the "full" season came.

One time I started a pizza delivery company, which provided some income for us while I helped a church I was active in, and I could be flexible with my hours as well. The plan was to become full-time with the church as pastor within a few months. I began the pizza delivery store in November of one year and God blessed the thing. Our first week we had $4,000 in cash sales and we got up to about $15,000 in cash sales very quickly—and pizza is a high profit business.

In April the following year, just six months later, I was praying and I heard the Father say this:

"You've learned what I wanted you to learn. Now I want you to sell it."

In the Father's mind the reason he had me start the business was to learn something; in my mind it was to make money. The Father holds the seasons in his own mind, in his own plans, in his own wisdom. As a Christian I gave up my right to set my own seasons.

My thoughts were about growth and expansion! The business was only six months old. Think about how much money I could make for the Lord, which would fund all kinds of good projects. "You've learned what I wanted you to learn. Now I want you to sell it." He is interested in the learning process, and to him, jobs, careers, houses and living locations are interchangeable and subject to his higher purposes. That is contrary to the un-renewed mind.

I waited a year before I sold the business and the sale barely covered the debts; I walked away with next to nothing. He told me to sell it in April and I disobeyed. By July, sales had started to decline. A competitor made further inroads into sales. If I had sold it at the time I was told to, I would have had enough money to at least put in the bank and help support us in ministry after the debts had been paid off. I missed heaven's season because I wanted to run my life according to my seasons. Eventually it cost a house to foreclosure, and a car to repossession.

If only I had done what the Lord said and realized the six months was a season, even though it didn't make sense in my brain. Jesus is saying in this passage, "My time is not yet. Your time is always." I was acting like an unbeliever, because I was not aware that there are seasons, lessons, and specifically set times that the Father has in mind for you and I, which he holds within his own knowledge. The beauty and purpose isn't revealed until the maturity of the season.

One thing that we can do in the season is ask the Father, "What is your purpose for the season that I'm in?" We know it's going to be for training according to Ecclesiastes, chapter 3. How do you handle the season? Do you overcome the frustration? Do you deal with the anger? Do you deal with the constraints placed upon you? How do you handle the frustration of knowing that your destiny lies somewhere else and this is just temporary? How do you conduct yourself with tact and diplomacy when the employer is hoping you're going to be there for fifty years and yet you have in your spirit that you're going to be in a foreign field someday? Or that you're going to be helping in church some way? It's how you deal with it that the Father observes and examines.

6

Angels Prepare, We Follow

We use to serve as pastors of a church; one night I was worshiping the Lord on my hands and knees in our 'great room' when I realized my hands were cupped around something. I opened my eyes and saw that my hands were holding the feet of Jesus! I noticed that the nails' scars were not like I had pictured them to be. Instead of healed over, like a modern doctor might take a flap of skin and cover the hole where the nail went in, he still had the holes, and the wall of the path of the nail through his feet was healed.

I looked up as I was still there crouching and saw that this time he was wearing a kind of sash over his robe that was about six to eight inches wide and ran from over his left shoulder and down to about his waist on his right side.

The sash was red and had some strange kind of writing on it that I could not read. It had to have been a very ancient, even primitive, language of straight vertical and horizontal lines and little slash lines. About the time I thought on these things, as I continued to look at the letters, the letters began to rearrange on his sash into English words that said, "The Word of God." When I looked away they reverted back to their original arrangement, and when I looked back at them they rearranged into English.

I realized that Revelation 19:13 says that at his return

he will be wearing clothing that had been dipped in blood and **"his name is called the Word of God."** I remember thinking that anyone of any language could look at what was written and understand it because the letters would rearrange into whatever language they were familiar with.

Jesus stepped back and to my left, and motioned with his left hand as he said:

"I have someone I would like to introduce to you. This is the angel in charge of your church. I want to teach you about spiritual warfare and how I start and shut down churches."

When he moved aside I discovered he had been obscuring my view because he was standing so close to me. When he stepped back I saw an angel that was about 10 or 11 feet tall standing in the middle of our 'great room.' His face and frame were larger than any man I had ever seen and he had a fierce countenance on his face. His complexion was the color of a penny and there was a sword on his belt. My wife is five feet three inches tall and I estimated that the sword blade was about five feet long and at least six inches wide with a handle about 12 inches long.

He began speaking and it sounded like the roar of Niagara Falls. I heard each word, but each word sounded like a waterfall it was so loud and with such authority. Again, it wasn't a roar like background sound, but each syllable was a roar of waterfall that rose and fell in pitch with each word. As his tongue, lips, and mouth formed each element of speech the roar fluctuated. It was both terrifying and fascinating.

For the first time in my life I experienced the fear of God on a personal level. The fear of God moved from the theological and theoretical into reality right then and there.

If Jesus hadn't been standing there I might have fainted.

I thought, "I'm a dead man."

As he told me that he was the angel in charge of the church, he also made it clear that his loyalty was not to me, but to the Lord and fulfilling his commands.

He said this was a rare opportunity for him to speak directly with the pastor of the church he was in charge of and assured me of his ability to do his job. He spoke to me about some people in the church: how the enemy was using them and how there were actually evil spirits speaking to them and stirring up trouble.

He also said, "If an evil spirit has authority in a church it is because the pastor has allowed it in, thus negating the authority of the angel of that church who would support the pastor's efforts to remove it. Oftentimes, a pastor will compromise with a spirit because he is afraid and the person controlled by the spirit gives money or holds a position of authority, either within a church or in the hearts of those in the congregation."

As he was telling me this he nearly bristled with indignation at the thought of a spirit entering into a church and him being powerless to stop it. As he continued to talk to me about a few of the people in the church I came to realize that angels must spend a lot of time trying to clean up pastors' mistakes.

I also realized he was just on assignment doing his job and he had no emotional attachment to me or the church, but that he loved his task of fighting the enemy forces and took a certain amount of personal pride and satisfaction in a job well done. He had a military bearing about him. The Lord told me about Exodus 23:20-21 when Israel came out of Egypt and an angel was to go before Israel:

"Behold, I send an angel before thee, to keep thee in the way, and to bring thee into the place which I have prepared. Beware of him, and obey his voice, provoke him not; for he will not pardon your transgressions: for my name is in him."

The Lord told me that angels are just on assignment and do not have the liberty to give people slack or forgive their laziness. As an example he referred me to Genesis 19 when the angels sent to rescue Lot made it very clear in verse 13:

"The Lord hath sent us to destroy it." But Lot lagged behind. Verse 16 says that **"while he lingered, the men (the angels) laid hold upon his hand, and upon the hand of his wife, and upon the hand of his two daughters; the Lord being merciful unto him: and they brought him forth, and set him without the city."**

They had a job to do and they didn't have the authority to change the plans. Remember, when they were in town rescuing Lot, Abraham had been interceding before the Lord to not destroy the city if he found ten righteous men. Evidently he didn't find ten and the Lord decided to follow through.

The angels couldn't tell the Lord, "We've decided to give Lot another week, so hold off." They were sent on a mission and they had to hurry the man and his family out of there!

After this, Lot asked the angels to allow him to go into a small city nearby instead of a mountain which they agreed to, but they added in verse 22: "I cannot do any thing till thou be come thither." Obviously their orders were to get him clear of the main destruction zone.

The Lord told me that many times provision is made for his people in accordance with their prayers and angels are sent to make it happen, but when time comes for them to step into what the Lord has done in the Spirit, people go their own way instead and get into trouble. He told me that many have even died because the angels prepared in one area but the people went in another direction, and the angels have to stick to their assignment and can't rescue people in these cases.

He showed me an example of what he was talking about. Suddenly we were standing in the air looking down into a church; I saw below us a young, single woman with two children sitting on the back pew. She was listening to the sermon, but her mind wasn't on the sermon and I heard her thinking to the Lord about some answers she needed.

One child appeared to be about three or so and the other was a baby. The three-year-old was standing up looking over the back of the pew and the baby was in her lap. I heard her prayers and thoughts as she ignored the sermon and complained to the Lord about her situation.

The Lord explained that her husband had left her and she was living with her parents, which is why she was in that church. He said she hadn't gotten a job yet and her car was broken down (he said it was the alternator). In her mind she was saying things like: "Lord, you said you'd be the Father to the fatherless, but look at my kids, where have you been faithful to them? Why have you abandoned me? Where is your provision? How am I going to get a job without a car and how can I get the car fixed without a job? This isn't mom and dad's problem; I can't keep sponging off them. Show me how to get my life and finances back in order…" And many other things like that.

My heart went out to this young mother who was thinking the Lord had abandoned her and she couldn't understand why he was allowing this difficulty. Then I turned to my left to ask the Lord what could be done, but what I saw stopped the words in my throat: Tears were streaming down his face as he heard what she was saying.

He said, "She is in this church because of loyalty to her parents, but she knows she is supposed to be going to another church." Just then I saw a church to our left, that was across town and a pastor delivering a message to his congregation that I heard this woman asking the Lord about. Jesus said he was teaching a series on finances and establishing God's order in life. She should have been in that other church getting her answers!

He said that beyond her, her children had a call on their lives that was being delayed and stifled because of her emotional unwillingness to do what was right.

He said, "She is seeking answers, and I have provided the answers but she is looking in the wrong place. He turned to the church across town and pointed out a man in a T-shirt sitting towards the front left. He said, "Do you see this man? He is a mechanic. I have commanded him to fix her car." He pointed out one older woman sitting with two friends: "Do you see this lady? She baby sits children in her home and I have commanded that she watch her children." Then he pointed out another man. "Do you see this man? He own a business in the town that has an opening for a receptionist, and I have commanded he give her that job."

I was reminded of Elijah and the widow of Zarephath in I Kings 17:8-16. In verse 9 the Lord told Elijah that he had commanded a widow to sustain him, but when he got there the lady was preparing what she thought was her last meal, completely unaware a miraculous provision had been commanded from heaven. She was ready to die not knowing the blessing had been commanded. This was exactly the case with this young mother I was observing.

Suddenly I saw off to our left, at about a forty-five degree angle, what appeared to be something of an assembly line. It was like a pathway into the future and there were angels at either side of this path. There wasn't a conveyor belt or anything like that, but I saw angels darting in and out of the path, while some stood on the side arranging things.

Jesus said, "This is my will for her for the next two years. The angels have prepared a job for her as I've said, and an apartment within two months; and I'm also sending her to school to complete her education. All this has been prepared for her to walk in."

Then off to our right I saw another path going two years into the future. Unlike the other path, which was lit by God's glory, this was dimly lit and had only one or two angels on the side looking rather inactive. Before I could ask what I was seeing he said, "This is the path she is heading down, which is outside my will. As soon as the command goes forth for the Father's will the angels are assigned to make ready everything needed. People will often start out along the right path, but when decisions that require growth or character are required they sometimes back off our perfect will and go their own way. This is what you are seeing. I am faithful and will do what I can, but the angels respond to the command in the perfect will of the Father and cannot change assignments at their will to excuse people's disobedience. We will not be blamed on the final day of judgment: when all is revealed everyone will see we have faithfully kept their words of commitment to us."

He said that sometimes these mistakes are evident quickly, other times it may take months or years before the person realizes they missed God and haven't been seeing his provision. He said they know in their spirits something is wrong, but most often they try to figure it out with their minds.

The Lord then brought up something that had happened early in our married life to drive the point home. My wife and I felt led to move to a particular city in September. My head reasoned that moving in May would be better. It would be springtime, rental properties would be more available, and the timing was good for us, so I made the decision and moved us and our six-month-old son there in May.

Nothing opened up for ministry. No church needed a pastor; I found myself working two jobs to help make ends meet, and the duplex we found to rent was very much below the standard where I wanted to move my young family.

In early June, my wife came home from a Bible study and left our son in the car while she went to open up the house. She soon realized she had not taken her house keys with her and was locked out of the house. She went around to the back and found the bathroom window over the shower and tub open, and crawled through.

While sitting on the windowsill she put out her hand to grab the shower curtain rod, supposing it to be a sturdy grip by which to swing down to the floor. As she put her weight on the bar (it was only held up by the tension on the bar and not fastened into the wall) it gave way and she fell head first, hitting her right cheek on the toilet seat with the full weight of her body behind her. This shattered her right cheek, right eye socket, and she had two skull fractures radiating over the right side of her head.

As she strugged to maintain consciousness, she remembered our six-month old son, Chris, still in his car seat in the back seat of our car on a sunny 80 degree day. She managed to stumble next door to find that our neighbors didn't speak English. Fortunately, she was able to communicate to them about Chris in the car and then dialed 911 herself before she collapsed.

Reconstructive surgery repaired the eye socket and cheek bone, but the doctor said she would have double vision, blurred vision, and complete numbness over the right side of her face, like a stroke victim because the main channel for the nerves on the right side was completely shattered. He told us that at the outside chance it might grow back (nerves are the slowest growing thing in the body), but it would be at least six months before any sensation would be noticed, and that full feeling would never return.

To Barb's credit she refused this prognosis and we set her up with tapes on healing and gave thanks continually for his healing power. She slept very little the first week and every waking moment was spent thanking and praising God for his healing power. Within seven days feeling started to return, and within 30 days she had normal feeling and was 100 percent restored. The doctor was amazed and had never seen anything like it. To this day, 20-plus years later, she has never had blurred or double vision and her face feels and functions normally.

The Lord reminded me that he had very clearly led us to move in September, not May. In September a church called who needed a pastor. It was part-time, but another job opened up with a Christian company and things began falling into place.

Between May and September all my praying and speaking the Word didn't change our lives one bit, but when early September came, everything fell into place. He told me that my angel had arranged everything for September, and he could not change his assignment or forgive my disobedience. Barb and my young son had nearly died because I had not obeyed the voice of the Lord and moved in his timing.

Once the depth of this had settled in, I asked the Lord for scripture that supported the concept that there are angels assigned to churches and that he could shut churches down. He told me Revelation 1:20:

"The mystery of the seven stars which thou sawest in my right hand, and the seven golden candlesticks. The seven stars <u>are the angels of the seven churches:</u> and <u>the seven candlesticks which thou sawest are the seven churches.</u>"

He also gave me Revelation 2:5: **"Remember therefore from whence thou art fallen, and repent and do the first works; or else I will come unto thee quickly, and will remove thy candlestick** [church] **out**

of his place [shut down], **except thou repent."**

He said this is the whole concept running throughout chapters two and three, **"to the angel of the church in..."** I told him there are different ways to interpret the word translated 'angel' and that some said it meant the pastor of that church. He looked at me kind of funny and said kindly but firmly:

"I am the one who spoke that message to the churches and I'm telling you how I intended it."

That stopped my questions, as I could tell he wanted to get on with the teaching.

As he began to speak we were in the spirit and I saw a group of three ladies in a small Colorado town on the eastern plains, meeting to pray for a good solid church and pastor for their community. The Lord said they relied on satellite programs and publications, but longed for a local church in accordance with their faith. He added that he had many people in that town.

We were observing them praying and I saw their prayers instantly reach the Father at his throne; I also saw that their desire for a church had actually originated with him, but they didn't realize it. Just as instantly he decided to answer their prayer, which, of course, had originated with him. He was just waiting for time to catch up with his plans that he'd had for them since before the beginning of the world. (II Timothy 1:9)

The principle is that whatever is bound or loosed on earth is bound or loosed in heaven. The Father wanted to provide a church, but he needed the ladies to ask him for one.

As they did so he was released to bring it to pass.

As I was watching this, the Lord told me that most intercessory prayer actually begins in heaven with the Father expressing a need. Sensitive people begin praying, sometimes aware this is what heaven wants and sometimes not. Their prayer on earth then releases the Father to get involved in earth and send the answer.

He also said there is a lot of intercessory prayer that happens in the flesh. People usually have a good heart, but are ignorant of how the spirit realm truly works. He said that for now, the Father is the one who sends angels—man is not yet authorized to send them. There will be a day we will rule over them, but it is not yet. He referred me to what he said in the garden of Gethsemane in Matthew 26:53:

"<u>Thinkest thou that I cannot now pray to my Father</u>, and <u>he shall presently give me</u> more than twelve legions of angels?"

He said that even he, in the days of his flesh would have had to ask the Father for angels and there is no example of anyone commanding angels to do this or do that.

I said "Yes, but Psalm 103:20 says they hearken to the voice of his word."

He said, "They do, and there are times when my people pray and speak the word and the angels are sent in accordance with that word, but I am talking about those that are in the flesh. That is, those who try to command angels to go here and there while they don't know what they are praying. My word says that you don't even know how to pray as you should (Rom 8:26), so what makes you think you know how to command angels and tell them what they need to do? Intercessors must be operating in the Spirit in order to receive the knowledge of how to pray and speak my word, then the angels are released."

"When we decide to start a church, we begin training and/or speaking to a pastor about coming to that town, or about the call to pastor."

Immediately I saw a man and his wife in another city and state in a Bible school. All this was going on at the same time: Jesus and I were standing in the air looking down at these three ladies praying to our left; at the same time seeing the Father on his throne answering their prayers directly in front and above us; and to our right and below this future pastor was in Bible school. The man knew he was called to pastor but he didn't know where, he just sensed in his spirit it was a small town, rural atmosphere in the west.

My attention would shift back and forth between the ladies praying some 700 miles or so away and this man in school. He was working long hours doing menial work while holding inside himself that he was a pastor, not a janitor.

Jesus was especially pleased with the way this man held the higher truth of his call within his heart and kept it alive by thinking about it and communing with the Lord. He submitted to the job the Lord had provided him and used his time to meditate on what he was learning and keep his heart right.

The Lord told me their budget was very tight and their stress level was high, but that they needed the training because of what they were called to do. He was pleased that they remained teachable and sensed this was a training time. He said, "Many of those called into full-time ministry don't understand that training involves character, too, not just Bible study."

They sensed this, but there were times they were tired. I saw them around their kitchen table going over the bills and praying for extra money and seeking wisdom on what to pay first. The man kept going back to what he knew inside he was called to do. His wife encouraged him, although she kept the checkbook and was concerned, but she was determined.

As I was watching this I looked to my left and saw one of the ladies go to the other two and talk to them about stopping their weekly prayer meeting and just accept that there would be no good church in their town. The other ladies wouldn't hear of it and encouraged her to hang in there with them because God would surely answer their prayers.

Jesus told me they had been praying 'about three years,' not realizing the Father had already answered their prayers and was preparing their pastor in another state. He said it took about a year for the man to answer the call in his spirit, and then it took a couple of years of school and character building to prepare him.

Jesus said to me, "When we decide to start a church an angel is assigned to the church and area it is to influence. His job includes preparing for the new pastor and sometimes includes helping that pastor get to his assignment even if he is out of state. This includes finances, housing, a job oftentimes, transportation, and preparing the hearts of the people to receive him."

When he said, "...and preparing the hearts of the people

to receive him," I instantly saw people in various walks of life in and around this town that the Lord began speaking to their hearts about desiring a good local church. I saw a rancher outside working on a fence who thought about this. I saw a man behind a counter at a store having the same thought. I saw men and women all having a desire and witness in their spirit to see a new church raised up. I saw some in churches the Lord said they weren't assigned to—dead churches, but they went there because there wasn't any other place to go, but when the new church started up they would go there by the Spirit, assigned by the Lord.

"If I decide to shut a church down the angel is reassigned elsewhere and the anointing lifts from off that work. I have shut it down. However, there are some churches still meeting today even though in the Spirit they have been shut down five, ten, even 50 years ago."

At this point he used a church in another town near our city as an example. At one time this church had been a thriving church and a leader in the immediate communities. Then they got into the "shepherding" movement to the point that people couldn't get jobs, change jobs, buy or sell cars and the like without the church leadership approval.

After that several couples in the leadership got caught up in adultery, two of the couples got divorced, and the pastor moved out of state. An older woman in the church actually owned the building and a handful of people remained with a new pastor they hired who had come in from out of town. This man was not called into full time ministry, but he desperately wanted to be in the ministry. He was actually called to helps, but was trying to pastor the church.

Jesus told me, "These people are still meeting weekly

even though I shut down the church and reassigned the angel long ago. Most of those people have been assigned to your church and you will see them make the move in the spring [this was October]. They can't figure out how to make their church grow and don't know what to do. They know there is no anointing but it will take awhile for them to become brave enough to shut it down. I am patient because there are those who are truly seeking me and don't understand what has happened.

"There are also many who start churches that I have not ordained to be started and there is no angelic covering, which provides the anointing for that church."

At this point, he reminded me of my first experience as a pastor. A leadership group of three men had hired me because they had started a church, which met in a trailer park clubhouse and had about six families or so.

I worked a regular job, but about half of my income was from the Sunday services and Wednesday Bible studies I led for the church. We seemed to never be able to get above those original families who started the church. Visitors would come and go and we would never see them again.

I would teach, but it seemed the anointing would go about five feet out from my mouth and fall to the ground.

Finally after about six months of this I really wanted to have some answers, so I spent three days eating light lunches and spending my lunch hour in prayer. On the third day, a Thursday, the Lord spoke to me:

"I did not ordain this church to be started. They started the church because they got in strife with their pastor and left their church. I want you to shut it down and tell the people I have churches for them to go to."

And that's exactly what I did the next Sunday morning. I found out that as Baptists they had gotten baptized with the Holy Spirit and soon knew more than their pastor. They watched him vary his stance on the Holy Spirit from all for it to totally against it depending on whether he had been influenced that week by his denomination or a charismatic TV ministry or convention he had attended. We left on good terms and remain so to this day. They went into established charismatic churches and serve those pastors in peace and full support.

You see, the angel represents the anointing of God for the church to exist. How terrible when a man or woman just decide they are going to start a church without the Lord actually initiating it! How the people open themselves and their congregation to error and spiritual attack!

Once, two ladies in a church we were pastoring decided they would go off and start their own church. They called everyone in the church directory and split the church. Some went to their 'church' but some came back because they said they tried to force the gifts of the Spirit into operation and 'something didn't feel right in the Spirit.' It takes many forms, but this and the church I shut down are common examples of churches starting on earth without ever having been started from heaven.

Of the above example, these ladies wore the spiritual 'pants' in their families and dominated their husbands, who were weak Christians and not very involved. Jesus told me:

"The relationship a person has with their church is

much like the relationship they have in marriage. Because these two ladies wear the pants in the family and control their husbands, as church members they will try to control the pastor. They will try to wear the pants in the church—they want to control the church as they control their marriage and won't settle for anything less. As Christians, they want to wear the pants in their relationship with me and control my plans for them."

He continued, "Usually the pastor's marriage is in proper order and this spirit can't take control over the pastor's wife, so she becomes the focus of the attack. The pastor must stand up against this spirit firmly, even at the risk of splitting the church, although many pastors call a truce with the spirit giving it a certain amount of room to operate within the church. When this happens, this means a pastor's wife lives in a constant tension and is often miserable...all the while her husband, the pastor, knows this. He honors another woman or women above his wife."

As he was saying this, his words were spoken in quite an angry tone towards the husband/pastor.

"A church like this is of little use to me, although I will bless it as much as I am able for the sake of the people, though they have effectively capped their growth in me and as a church."

This shed additional light on what the angel had told me from his perspective: that if a spirit is in a church, it is because of the pastor. How little I knew of their perspective in the spirit realm and how much I wanted to know!

We then went back to watching this pastor as time came for him to graduate. The experience was a series of highlights from about a two-year period, all shown to me in a few minutes. I knew I was seeing some past event and some future events during this narration.

I watched him gradually progress from going through files of requests (for pastors) from churches and communities to him settling in the town where the ladies had been praying. I wanted to jump in at various points and tell him I knew where he was to go and tell the ladies their pastor was on his way, but I could only observe! Eventually I saw him move with his family to that town where the ladies had been praying. Jesus continued:

"When the pastor moves into town and begins the church, the burden of intercession shifts to him. It is important for the intercessors to realize they were just the tools used to bring him in and they deserve no credit for starting the church. Sometimes an intercessor or group of intercessors will never truly give the pastor authority in their hearts to be their pastor. They think of themselves as being the real power in the church. This is pride and error. Many prayer groups get off into doctrinal error and get what you would call 'flaky.' It begins with pride and an unwillingness to give place of control in their hearts over to the pastor I have chosen. Therefore their problem is with me, not the pastor, although they will attack him."

At this point Jesus and I were suddenly in the living room of a lady who was one of our main intercessors, although she was very independent and at times had gotten a little weird. At one point the Spirit told me to bring her prayer meeting in to the church, not in her or other's houses because she was getting out from under the covering of the church in her heart. Jesus said it was for her protection because she was straying in her heart and fancied herself as a pillar in the intercessory community. This caused some consternation on her part when I asked her to meet in the church, but she did it.

Then about four weeks after this the Lord told me to sit in on her prayer meetings in the church because she was getting off, spiritually. I began attending and found out she was giving "names" to all the higher spirits over our state and was calling on them by name to be cast down.

These weren't names that described what they were, which is the gospel example—for example the spirit of infirmity, deaf spirit, and so on—she was calling them elaborate personal names. I had to instruct her that she was in error, which she received on the surface, but not in her heart.

Suddenly Jesus and I were in her living room and she was ranting and raving to someone on the phone she was angry with. Jesus was on my left observing and narrating. She cursed and slammed the phone down and I saw the motives of her heart by the Spirit: she wanted control and when she didn't get it she was furious.

Jesus said that was how she felt toward me and I needed to cast that spirit out of my church. (Not her human spirit, but the evil spirit controlling her.) Instantly we were back in my house and I took authority over the spirit operating through her and commanded it to leave my church. About three weeks later this woman came to me and said the Lord was leading her to leave the church.

Back in my house he spoke to me about the effects in satan's realm when a church begins affecting a community. He said, "When a new church moves into an area, or when a church begins to truly influence the people in their community, evil spirits are displaced. Like the woman we have just visited, either she gets delivered from the spirit or she won't come near that church. You have read in Mark 5:10 that Legion asked me not to send them all out of that country, or region. They don't want to leave the area they are used to. They know the people there and have their territories established.

"When people begin getting born again and living for me those spirits find that they no longer have influence and they look for other areas. Sometimes they will be displaced into other demons' areas, which cause turmoil and confusion in their realms. There is a momentum in a church that develops when my people can sense by the Spirit that their area is being cleansed from the evil spirits previously assigned there. Crime rates will drop, my blessing will be on my people, their work and possessions, and even those who don't know me will benefit. These things I do often."

He began talking to me about a husband and wife who were members of my church. They had a heart for outreach to the poor and transient population in our area and headed up this outreach for our church. The husband was gifted with the guitar and they loved bringing food and music to those in need. At some point they became offended at some people in the church and their attendance became less frequent.

I visited with them and encouraged them to stay strong and walk in love, but they were in the midst of deciding whether or not to return to church. Jesus told me:

"Yours is the tenth fellowship [before there was a church] or church they have been a part of and have left because of offense or they didn't get their own way. This is their last chance. If they do not submit to my dealing with them and make the right decision they will never again be allowed to be a part of any ministry in this area and will spend the rest of their days wandering the valley [our town was in a valley] from church to church and special meeting to special meeting, never finding a place to rest."

He talked about people who need to grow up in him, put away pride and selfishness, and settle into the church the Lord has provided for them. Much of the time the trouble is that people still want to be taught when in fact they should be teaching and active leaders in the church.

There was a time I had been a pastor at a church for about six months and wanted to make some changes in the worship team. They were accustomed to being pretty laid back when they played during the worship services on Wednesday and Sunday—wearing jeans, work jackets and boots, or whatever clothes they had on at work. I asked them to change clothes and wear something more presentable. They all got angry with me and said I was just like pastor X, who was the pastor two pastors ago. They quit immediately and left the church without a worship team!

In prayer the Lord told me, "You have been the pastor now for six months and I have given them space to grow, but they have not, therefore their problem is with me not with you. Don't pay any attention to them, their problem is with me, and I will deal with it."

The Lord raised up another leader and team that was very anointed and served us well for the duration of our time there!

7

Friend of God

The Lord is looking for disciples, yes, servants, yes, ambassadors, yes, but the result of three years of ministry with his disciples was that he called them "friends."

In John 15:14, Jesus said:

"You are my friends, <u>if ye do whatsoever I command you.</u>" Verse 15: "...I have called you friends; <u>for all things that I have heard of my Father I have made known unto you.</u>"

Friendship with the Lord involves doing what he tells us **and** being in a position to have him reveal things of the Father to us. Too many want to experience great and wonderful revelations of the Lord without being a doer of what he tells them.

Jesus Desires Friendship

The Lord had just finished speaking to me about how he starts and shuts down churches, and he turned and started to walk away from me, like he was going to another part of the house. I knew from experience that within a step or two he would disappear from sight. I asked him as he turned, "Lord, why are you appearing to ME to teach ME these things?" He stopped, turned around, took a step towards me and paused as he looked down at the ground in thought for a second or two. Then, with a tilt of his head and a puzzled look on his face that seemed to say 'you know the answer' he replied:

"Because you are my friend."

There were several seconds of silence between us as I stared into his eyes trying to comprehend the depth of what he was saying, and wrestle with my own arguments at the same time.

As I stared at him I was thinking, "Who am I that I should be visited by my Lord?" But my arguments were overcome with the overwhelming awareness of aspects of his personality flowing from him that I had never seen before: Loneliness and sorrow.

His eyes spoke of a deep desire for fellowship and a sorrow for his children that don't walk in all he has for them. He was especially sad about those members of his body who were caught up in, and living like, the world. It wasn't a hurt, but a sorrow that he had done so much for them and they treated what he had done with so little respect, distracting them with this present world.

My wife and I had given up much for the Lord and the Gospel's sake and had endured many hardships as a result, and there was a sense of kinship and fellowship between us. He appreciated what we had endured for his sake and there was a sense of commonality between us due to the hardships endured and battles won. Paul's words of Philippians 3:10 rang out:

"That I may know him, and the power of his resurrection, and the <u>fellowship of his sufferings,</u> being made conformable unto his death."

There is a "fellowship of his sufferings"—a sharing and appreciation that can only be shared by those who have endured similar difficulties. I experienced camaraderie with him like I never had before. For the first time, I knew he appreciated what I had gone through and he could relate to me in this way because of hardships he had endured. Similarly, it was the first time I had ever viewed the everyday hardships I endured as having an eternal value and appreciation from him.

I then asked him something I had never asked in all my prayers and all my praise and worship to him over the years.

"Lord, what is it you desire? What is on your heart?"

He replied, "I enjoy it when my people just like being with me, not asking anything of me, just enjoying me, for it is then that we enter into true communion and fellowship. This is my great desire: fellowship, to be with my people, that my people would enjoy me for just being me, this is true worship."

Suddenly I realized that relatively few Christians truly know the Lord. They pray like they place an order at a restaurant: Here is a list of things I need or want, Amen. Sometimes they pray to wage spiritual warfare—there is a job to be done—and yet other times they enter into praise and worship with the ulterior motive of getting something from him. Some use praise and worship as a formula and means manipulating an answer from the Lord. Many don't want to live right, but want all the benefits of the Life of God to be manifest in their lives.

Walking with the Lord

Genesis 5:24 says that Enoch

"walked with God."

Hebrews 11:5 says that Enoch

"had this testimony, that he pleased God."

He walked with God; this pleased God.

Walking with the Lord as a close friend is highly valued by the Lord.

Walking with the Lord means you choose to talk to him as you would a friend. You choose talking to him over listening to the radio station or CD player in the car. You spontaneously thank him for a beautiful sunrise or blooming flower and he speaks back as one would share with a close friend. This is the realm of true fellowship.

One day on my way to work, as I admired the beautiful morning, the Lord said, "There are wild turkeys crossing your land now." When I got to work I called my wife and told her. Two days later she looked out the kitchen window to our west pasture just in time to see a flock of turkeys come out of the woods. I didn't ask for that information, I was just enjoying him, and he volunteered it.

Another day as I was driving into work I realized it was the time of day the local Christian station played an album from start to finish. I thought, "I wonder what they're playing today?" not really directing it heavenward. Instantly I heard back, "The 2nd Chapter of Acts, *The Roar of Love* album; they're just starting side two." I worshiped him for his goodness and turned on the radio a couple of minutes later just in time to hear my favorite song from the album.

There is another aspect to friendship with the Lord that Jesus shared with me that day: **Friends keep confidences.**

He shared that although many people have wonderful experiences in the things of the Spirit, they get puffed up, or they don't learn what he intended for them to learn, or they get into the flesh and change it or otherwise err, so he limits what he tells them. I thought of Mark 4:24 that says, "Be careful how you hear, for with the measure [value] you place on what you hear, that is how it will be measured back to you."

Jesus continued:

"Others receive information from me in these times of fellowship or prayer and they share it with others, thus cheapening something I intended to be just between us. They have violated the intimacy we shared in that moment. I test my people sometimes in this way, seeing how they value true intimacy with me. For many say they want to be close to me, and truly they draw close for a time, but when I share something of a private nature with them and then they share it with others, they have proven themselves unworthy of such intimacy."

Many people won't walk in what is revealed in black and white in their Bible, but want to move in spontaneous ways in the spirit; but it isn't going to happen. When we walk in the light we have, then he will begin speaking to us about "spontaneous" things.

I John 1:9 is a verse most of us know.

"If we confess our sins, <u>he is faithful</u> and just to forgive us our sins, and to cleanse us from all unrighteousness."

One day as I was driving home I was thanking the Lord for forgiving me: "Thank you, Lord, for being faithful to me and forgiving me…" The Father interrupted my prayer:

"I'm not being faithful to you, I'm being faithful to the work of my son on the cross."

At first that devastated me. All along I thought that when I confessed my sin and the Lord forgave me, he was being faithful to me and the call on my life. Now I saw that I am not a factor at all! The Father is being true to his son's work on the cross, not me at all! Now I was elated. That ended all my groveling and sense of "here we go again, Lord," while battling in my mind that one of these days he's going to say, "That's it, I've had it, I'm not forgiving this one!"

Suddenly I saw that his grace was much bigger than weighing it out on a case-by-case basis. All he saw was that his son had covered it all, so he forgave me based on that! What freedom—not to sin—but to walk in fellowship.

Since that day, when satan comes with a temptation I

don't stand against it based on fear or double-mindedness, but rather, "Why would I want to break this wonderful fellowship with the Lord?" And suddenly the temptation pales in the face of the beauty of the fellowship and presence of the Lord. I suddenly had the freedom NOT to sin, not to break that sweet fellowship of the Spirit.

I John 1:7 says:

"...<u>if we walk in the light</u>, as he is in the light, <u>we have fellowship</u> one with another, and <u>the blood of Jesus Christ his Son cleanseth us</u> from all sin."

This is saying that if you walk in the light of what you know—that is, to say you are walking uprightly before him and in fellowship one with another—then the blood of Jesus "cleanses" us continually; it's an ongoing action.

Think back a few months or years ago when you saw a movie. You thought it was a pretty good movie. Then you saw it a couple of years later and thought: "How could I have thought that was a good movie? Look at all the filth in it." Did the movie change? No, you did. Where you were with the Lord then was a place of less maturity, and even though that movie still grieved the spirit and was sin, he "cleansed" you because you continued in fellowship with him and were walking in the light you knew at the time. It's an ongoing process when we walk honestly before him.

Friendship with the Lord is the key to intimacy with him. Intimacy with him produces miracles in our lives. The reward is great. The trials and tribulations we undergo on earth, when handled correctly, build gold, silver, and precious stones in heaven. Walk with the Lord. Be his friend!

Heaven's Value System

I was at church on a Sunday night. There was an altar call—a call for repentance—and seven people came down. Six people had their heads bowed in silent contemplation as the pastor was addressing the congregation.

There was a man in the middle of the line who had his arms upraised, his upturned face beaming with joy as he gently moved the upper part of his body back and forth as if to some heavenly rhythm.

I had seen him before; he was a deaf and mute man who often participated in altar calls, but this was the first time I had seen him exhibit such joy. His joy and actions were out of place for the type of altar call, and I was drawn to watching him.

As I watched, I suddenly saw a shaft of light coming down from the ceiling aimed at and hitting him in the head, but it was more than just hitting him in the head, his head was inside the shaft and it stayed on him no matter how he turned. I could see that there was a direct correlation between his joy and that shaft of light. As my eyes traced the light up towards the ceiling area (about 30 feet up) I saw words flowing from the Father down the beam of light and into this man.

Suddenly I found myself eavesdropping by divine revelation on words of love flowing from the Father to this man. I both read and heard the words. In part, He was telling him how much he was loved and appreciated. The Father was telling the man He saw his hard work and was pleased. He was sending love that was tangible into this man. Though he is mute, I'm sure if he could have shouted he would have: his mouth was open, he had a huge grin across his face, and he could barely contain himself for the joy and love that was coursing through him.

The Father continued, "My son, you have a throne and authority in my kingdom. I have provided great things for you and you shall walk in them, for you have been faithful in your love for me."

As I witnessed this I blurted out in my mind, "Father, why him?" Just as quickly the Father responded, "Because of the simplicity of his love for me. His love for me is unencumbered with ulterior motives and he asks nothing for himself. The purity of his love for me is uncomplicated by issues others are distracted with. It is because of the simplicity and purity of his love that I bless him this way. In the ages to come he will share the wisdom which flows from this simplicity and purity of love."

I asked, "You've given him a throne and authority?" Again he responded, "He has been given authority because he has done more with the little he has been given in this life than nearly everyone here [in the church that night] whom you would consider "whole." Therefore he will be their teacher."

I asked, "Why don't you just heal him?" The Father replied very quickly and with a matter of fact tone, "I enjoy his worship."

"But Father," I reasoned, "he's missing so much of life he could have if he was healed—family, jobs, cars, and so on." He replied, "I make sure he has everything he needs. He finds his fulfillment in his love and fellowship with me."

"But what a wonderful testimony and example of love

he could be to everyone if you healed him, and he could tell us here in this life about loving you with purity and simplicity."

He continued teaching me, "They [the congregation] have the scripture that tells them what pure religion and love is, yet this man is not even given a thought or noticed by them. Therefore I have set him in their midst as an example and testimony to them, that by him they might know humility and simplicity of love for me. Learn wisdom in this, son, most just see a deaf mute, but I see a man who loves me in simplicity and purity, therefore he will be their teacher. Look at people as I see them, for man looks at the outward appearance, but I see the heart and weigh all things in the balance. Know people according to their heart."

8

The Reward

One day I was in prayer with my eyes closed, kneeling down at the front of the church with my hands partly raised in worship. Suddenly I saw an arm appear in the air just above me and to my left. It reached down and I heard the voice of my angel say:

"Take hold of my hand."

When I did so I saw my spirit's arm come up out of my physical arm and take hold of his hand. Just as soon as I did that I was pulled up and out of my body and we flew very fast through the roof of the church and out into space. It happened so quickly that we were in space before I thought to look back at the earth—and when I did I couldn't find it! All around us was the blackness of space with millions and millions of stars. There was no up or down or any way to gauge direction. I was perfectly comfortable and aware we were traveling very fast.

Flying through space isn't like you see in the movies and TV when spaceships hit light speed and all the stars become extended lines of light closely arranged to each other and close to the ship. The stars remained the same distance apart as they were when I observed them on earth. Though I felt we were traveling very fast, my view of the stars seemed to move at a barely perceptible rate.

I kept thinking that at some point I would get closer to them and they would all seem much closer and larger then, but it never happened. The distances are so vast in all directions that the change of my position as I flew through space was hardly noticeable—even though we must have traveled a huge distance. I was overwhelmed at how vast space was.

As I held onto his hand and looked around (I only had a few seconds to look) we suddenly began decelerating, and I looked ahead of me for the first time and remembered something my heavenly Father had told me shortly after I was born again at age 16.

One day he was teaching me some things and said, "When you get your glorified body, you will find it is not subject to the natural laws of the earth." I asked what he meant and he responded, "If you want to fly, you can fly. If you want to float, you can float. If you want to be somewhere, you can walk, run, or be there at the speed of thought." I knew I was not yet in a glorified body, that it was just my spirit and soul that have the same appearance as my body, but the effect was the same.

We were quickly approaching a city; our approach was from below and rising upwards. What a sight! Suspended in space was suddenly a huge wall about 20 stories high. Our approach was near one corner, so I was able to see one wall receding into the distance to my left and the other side of the wall receding into the distance on my right.

The wall was the most beautiful thing I had ever seen. The construction of it was the size, weight, and thickness of blocks of granite, but the material of the blocks seemed to have the translucency of giant, clear ice cubes or quartz, although the colors they gave off included a golden glow. All kinds of precious stones seemed to be imbedded in the blocks. There were layers of colors from the bottom up of greens and reds and blues primarily, but to gaze over it without focusing on one spot revealed a gold-white glory that seemed to emanate from everywhere.

There were colors that are beyond what our natural eyes can see. I became aware that our earth-eyes in their fallen state are not able to perceive the countless subtleties and variety of colors there really are. Everything was equally light without any shadow or lessening brightness of light, and the very molecular structure seemed to vibrate with life. It seemed my eyes had the ability to see not only the gold-white light, but I could see that within those colors the whole spectrum of seen and unseen light and multitudes of every possible hue and color combination existed and played off each other as we passed by.

The earthly city of Jerusalem has walls of worn, weathered stones. The city I saw was many, many times larger and the walls were adorned with all kinds of precious stones. And the construction of the heavenly was perfect: every corner met precisely and every line was perfectly aligned with another. The precious stones seemed to have been cut with styles that were different—for the most part—than what we see today in jewelry stores, and their quality made them look almost extruded they were so smooth and so well placed as part of the wall.

The change in my eyesight was noticeable immediately. If I wanted to look at something in the far distance, instantly I could see like I was standing right there, in as little or as much detail as I wanted, just like when I looked into Jesus' eyes in Mexico. I scanned down one wall and could see all the way to the end in detail!

The Bible says in Revelation 21:16 that the walls are about 1,500 miles long, or about halfway across the United States, yet I could examine each gate as we were flying by just by looking down the wall.

As we flew up and over the wall—we didn't use one of the gates of pearl, which seemed to be placed about every 300 miles apart or so along each side (I appreciated the symmetry and neatness immediately)—I saw that the city had the look of antiquity in style, yet nothing needed fixed up or repaired. There was no aging or weathering on the building or walls or streets. It looked brand new and immaculate in every detail, yet I knew it was ancient.

I saw the skyline as we flew over. It seemed to be a mixture of every architectural style I had ever seen, but basically it was a middle-eastern city, and reminded me of postcards I had seen of the wall of Jerusalem looking into the city with the sun setting behind the photographer and casting a golden glow on everything. Yet Jerusalem on earth was at best a very, very poor type and shadow of the glorious one I was sailing over.

It's important to understand the significance of the building of heaven. My wife, Barb, had a vision of heaven shortly after she was saved and saw her home there. She states:

"The sun was beginning to set as I was looking west out the window of an upstairs bedroom. As I was looking at the evening light suddenly the wall disappeared. It just dissolved away, and I was standing in another place.

"The first thing I noticed was the life. Everywhere, even in just the molecules in the air, there was life. I walked up a hill a little way and I remember there was a bit of a wall off to my right. There was beautiful music, like a soft background music that complimented the whole of heaven. There were gorgeous smells, and I found myself standing on a path. It was just a dirt path, and I looked up and there was a house in front of me.

"If you've ever seen the pyramids in Egypt you've noticed they're not made with mortar. At least by today there is no mortar visible. They're just fit together. The stones are fit together, and that's the way this house was. It was just made of stones fit together like that. And it was carved out. It was just a small house. We'd call it a bungalow. Maybe you could house one person in there. It had a doorway carved into the stones.

"The stones were all put together without mortar, but it had carved into it a place where a door would be. And on either side of the door was carved into it where two windows would be. And it was carved all in stone, even to the point where a roof would be, though there wasn't a roof on it yet.

"When you're in heaven you have spiritual eyes and you can see in dimensions and things that you can't see here on the earth. Even though I was looking at it, suddenly I could see down around and all the way back behind the house, and I saw down off to the side, there were some trees and it was beautiful. It was like a park. There's nothing dead in heaven. Everything's gorgeous. You're never going to have to take care of your lawn. You're never going to have to take care of the gardening. It's all taken care of.

"I was just standing there looking at this house and it was so gorgeous even though it was just stone, when I realized someone was standing next to me. It was Jesus. He said:

"'This is your new home in heaven, <u>and as you give us things to build with on the earth we will add to it here in heaven.</u>'"

Though Barb was just a newly born-again Christian with no Bible knowledge when she experienced this vision, the Word of God clearly teaches us about giving God things to build with. I Corinthians 3:9-15 says:

"...<u>ye are God's building</u>.
...I have laid the foundation, and another buildeth thereon. But let every man <u>take heed how he buildeth</u> thereupon.
For other foundation can no man lay than that is laid, which is Jesus Christ.
Now <u>if any man build upon this foundation</u> gold, silver, precious stones, wood, hay, stubble;
Every man's work shall be made manifest: for the day shall declare it, because it shall be revealed by fire; and the fire shall try every man's work of what sort it is.
If any man's work abide <u>which he hath built</u> thereupon, he shall receive a reward.
If any man's <u>work shall be burned</u>, he shall suffer loss: but he himself shall be saved; yet so as by fire."

There is further evidence in scripture (I Peter 2:5) that we give God material to work with:

"Ye also, as lively [living] **stones, are <u>built up</u> a spiritual house..."**

Realize that the sacrifices and difficulties you handle

in Christ are translated into building material for God! If we handle things incorrectly, we build wood, hay, and stubble, which will not survive the Judgment Seat of Christ, though we ourselves will. If we mature and grow in the things of God, those victories add heavenly material to our spiritual house. We build gold, silver, and precious stones, which will survive the fire of his judgment.

This sounds amazing and beyond our comprehension, but consider what the angel told Cornelius in Acts 10:4:

"...Thy prayers and thine alms <u>are come up for a memorial before God.</u>"

A memorial is something built to commemorate a noteworthy event, a battle, gallant sacrifice, or noble heroism such as we see in our nation's capital and city squares around the country. Though Cornelius gave "much alms to the people," there were no earthly memorials to commemorate his gifts of sacrifice and love, so God built a memorial in heaven to him! How the Lord took prayers, and money, and translated them into a memorial in heaven we don't know, but the Lord has done this throughout the ages. Note David's words in Psalm 56:8:

"...put thou <u>my tears into thy bottle</u>: are they not <u>in thy book</u>?"

David was saying God took all his tears of anguish and loss when he poured out his heart in prayer, and saved them in a heavenly bottle, and wrote them in a heavenly book of remembrance.

And what does Revelation 5:8 say of the scene around the throne of Almighty God?

"And when he had taken the book, the four beasts and four and twenty elders fell down before the Lamb, having every one of them harps, and golden vials [bottles] **full of odors** [incense]**, *which are the prayers of the saints.***"

There are times we may wonder if the Lord truly sees our sacrifice and crucifixion of the flesh as we serve him, but I can assure you, saint, that he sees! Cornelius' prayers and financial gifts came up as a memorial before the throne. The prayers of the saints are transformed into heavenly incense before the throne. This is why the Old Testament tabernacle had an altar of incense before the veil in front of the Holy of Holies—it was a type of the prayers of the priest and people. God has been transforming tears, gifts, anguish, and sacrifice into real, tangible spiritual material since man has been on the earth!

We know of the rainbow placed on the earth after Noah's flood as a sign of God's covenant, but did you know that God also made a rainbow and put it in heaven as a reminder of his promise? Rev 5:3 says:

"...and there was a rainbow about the throne, in sight like unto an emerald."

We may ask ourselves, "To what purpose does God take my life built on the foundation of Jesus and add gold, silver, and precious stones?" Or, "Why would he even want my sacrifices to be made into something?" It is because he is building something with it! He is building a city, which will be finished when we as the body of Christ "grow up into him in all things." He is waiting until his bride has given him enough building material to complete the city! Revelation 21:2, 9-11:

"And I, John, saw the holy city, new Jerusalem, coming down from God out of heaven, prepared as a bride adorned for her husband. Come hither, <u>I will show thee the bride, the Lamb's wife</u>. And he...<u>showed me that great city, the holy Jerusalem, descending out of heaven</u> from God, Having the glory of God: and her light was like unto a stone most precious, even like a jasper stone, clear as crystal..."

"I will show you the bride...and he showed me...the holy Jerusalem."

We are the bride, the lamb's wife, <u>the heavenly city</u>! Our victories and hard-fought maturity in Christ during this lifetime are being transformed into gold, silver, precious stones, and are being used as the construction materials the new Jerusalem is built with! Notice how the city walls are made with beautiful stones, and each of the 12 foundational stones are a memorial to the lives of the apostles as recorded in Revelation 21:14:

"And the wall of the city had twelve foundations, and in them the names of the twelve apostles of the Lamb."

He goes on to describe the different jewels and gold the wall and city is made with: all materials furnished by real men and women on earth who lived sold-out lives for God!

The foundation of the city is the corner stone, Jesus. His life, death, and resurrection form the very foundation the city (the bride) is founded upon. Built upon his life of sacrifice are the lives of the 12 apostles. Their lives furnished material to build strong walls around the city as they added "gold, silver, and precious stones." Your life, too, started with the foundation of Jesus Christ.

The question is: *What* have we built on that foundation? Have we given the Lord gold, silver, and precious stones, or wood, hay, and stubble? Are our lives filled with hidden motives and pride, or pure motives and love, even when it is extremely painful to endure the personal hardship and character building? Are we looking at this earthly, temporary existence? Or are we always mindful of the reward of heaven and a future day of judgment?

As Jesus said to the apostle John after he saw the city and its building materials in Revelation 22:12:

"And, behold, I come quickly; and my reward is with me, to give every man according as his work shall be."

The Lord also personalizes the material of our lives as we grow in him. I saw all the architectural styles of buildings the world has ever known, which made it a very interesting sight indeed! As we came up over the wall I could see rooflines and building types. I saw flat roofs like in the middle east and other dry areas of the world, onion domes and spires like in Russia and the middle-east, rounded roofs and pitched roofs like in the United States and west as well as row houses along the streets.

It occurred to me at one point that some of the houses looked like row houses you'd see in Philadelphia or New York: all had identical fronts with a common wall between them and identical steps leading up to each door. I remember thinking "I guess some people will get a surprise if they are expecting a mansion."

I remembered that the King James Version of John 14:2 says:

"In my Father's house are many <u>mansions</u>" and also 14:23: **"...and my Father will love him, and we will come unto him, and make our <u>abode</u> with him."**

As I was observing the houses, I remembered that the word translated "mansions" is the same word translated "abode" in verse 23. The translators couldn't see King James living in a house, so they inserted "mansions" instead. That's not to say there aren't mansions, it just struck me that I didn't see any as we were flying over. Perhaps some didn't build well on the foundation of Jesus. The streets were very narrow; I thought to myself they were made for pedestrian traffic, not cars.

The main house area seemed to be fairly well concentrated in an area bordered by a couple of the walls and there was a lot of open, park-like area. I didn't see a lot of people walking around the streets coming and going to the houses. It seemed they were gathered around the throne, which was further back from the walls into the main part of the city.

We landed in a grassy area that seemed to be a kind of "green space" leading out into a completely natural setting as far as the eye could see ahead and to my left. The main part of the city and some of the houses we had flown over were to my right and behind a short wall that curved away from us in a soft "S."

My angel was standing to my right, and before us was about 50 feet of grassy area that led to a river flowing from my right to my left. It seemed to be about 30 feet wide and I asked my angel what it was. He said, "You would think of it as a branch of the River of Life that proceeds from the throne." I hadn't thought about it being divided into different streams, but I realized that the original design of the Garden of Eden was one river that divided into four separate ones.

The river seemed to be alive and full of energy. It was clear water that, at least in this section, seemed to make its own waves because it had so much life it could barely stay in its banks. As it flowed waves rose and fell in what I could only sense was joy!

When I looked at it joy and excitement rose up in me and I became almost giddy to the point I couldn't contain myself. When I looked away it subsided. I laughed out loud when I saw the waves jump and fall almost like they were playing with each other. Every molecule vibrated with life and a subtle harmony. The waves weren't breaking toward the riverbank—they were flowing downstream!

There was a very subtle but all pervasive music that seemed to be emanating from the grass, trees, water, wall, and every home and street. This isn't like elevator music or obnoxious restaurant music that you can tell by direction that it's coming from speakers in the ceiling. This music was the music of life that literally caused the molecules of grass to vibrate. The music didn't come from one source—it came from everything!

I looked straight up and the sky seemed to be a pinkish hue with a soft blue and other soft colors blended in. It seemed to be pastel shades that were lit with a light source from elsewhere. I couldn't tell where the light source was.

I looked at the grass and there wasn't anything dead

or mal-formed. The shades of green were beyond earthly green in richness and the hues were deeper and beyond what my earth eyes could detect in plants on earth. I bent over to examine the blades of grass because some varieties on earth can scratch and cut you, but these had a soft texture.

I straightened up and noticed trees about a quarter mile away by some grass-covered hills, and when I wanted to look at their leaves in detail I instantly saw with nearly microscopic ability every vein. Even though I was standing a quarter mile away, I could examine anything with detail only limited by my thoughts. That's how I know about the molecules. I don't know how to describe it, but I wanted to look closer at the leaves to test my eyes' ability and I was able to look at the cellular level. I saw the individual cells of the leaf vibrating with the life of God because they had so much life in them!

The grass seemed to be about a foot high where we were standing and there were flowers interspersed throughout, but most of the grass was about two feet high, especially on the other side of the river. At that point I noticed movement in the grass off to my right. There was something moving toward us at a fairly high rate of speed through the grass, but because the grass was two feet high or more it was covered mostly with the grass, so it made a kind of rustle and tunnel appearance as it came closer.

It came through the grass from my right, which was toward the main part of the city, and because the river had grass growing right to the water's edge it was only at the last second before it jumped over the river that I saw it was our golden retriever, Abby!

Abby had died about a year and a half earlier when she

had been hit by the school bus. I was just pulling out of the driveway and looked to my right and there she was lying on the side of the road as the bus continued on its route. I picked her up and we buried her in the back yard under some fruit trees.

It was a very difficult loss because our three boys were younger then and this was the first pet they had lost. It was also very hard on Barb, who, with three boys and a husband, really enjoyed Abby as the only other female in the house! Abby also kept watch over she and the boys when I was away and would wait up with Barb until I arrived back home.

We had prayed to the Lord for Abby to be in heaven; there were horses in heaven—Elijah was carried away in a chariot and Revelation 19:11,14 says Jesus and the saints will be riding horses at his return—so we used those examples in the Bible and "According to your faith be it unto you" spoken by Jesus so much in the gospels as our scripture references.

Abby looked wonderful! She nearly glowed and she was so clean and brushed out! She jumped the 30 feet of river without any apparent effort and sat down right in front of me like she was expecting bits of table scraps. I realized she could not have jumped 30 feet on earth and noted that she wasn't out of breath at all.

In addition to Abby, my little pet monkey, Tilly, was right along side her. My parents divorced when I was about twelve years old and my mom bought me a pet squirrel monkey about a year or so later. Squirrel monkeys can't use their tails to hold on to things and they are rather small, about ten inches tall. Tilly would stand with a foot on each side of the back of my neck and hold on to my hair as she peered over the top of my head to look forward as I would walk around.

After about a year she became very ill one day and as we rushed her to the veterinarian she died in my lap. The vet examined her and said she had a congenital intestinal defect that was not possible to detect. I buried her in the backyard all by myself. At that time in my life she was my closest friend.

When I was born again at age 16, one of the first things I did was ask the Father to have Tilly in heaven. I didn't know anything about horses being there, I just missed my little friend and wanted her to be there with me.

I was thrilled the Father had granted me that prayer, and Tilly seemed excited, too, as she ran to me like she used to and found her familiar perch on my neck and shoulders. Then, just as quickly, she jumped down and joined Abby sitting before me, although she seemed to be trying to get her to play by picking at her fur and not watching me at all.

As Abby looked at me with her tongue hanging out one side of her mouth (although she wasn't panting), and I looked at those big soulful eyes I suddenly understood her thought! She asked, "Where is Barb? And the boys?" I was startled that I suddenly knew what she just thought. I turned to look at my angel briefly because I was so surprised, but instantly I knew the answer as he told me, "In heaven you become much more a part of God's total knowledge and the way of life here is to flow in his knowledge."

Then I remembered that Adam named all the animals in the Garden of Eden. In the Hebrew culture and in the roots of the way we still name things, to name something is to know its character and nature. I realized Adam had a very intimate knowledge of the nature, habits, and ways of the animals and could therefore communicate with them beyond our fallen state.

I remembered, too, that the Jewish historian, Josephus, says that in the Garden of Eden all the animals originally spoke a common language (understood by Adam).

How often on earth I had wanted to know what Abby wanted when she stared us down in the living room. Did she want out? Did she want to play? Did she want more food or water? Now in heaven I discovered that what we would call a word of knowledge on earth was much more natural and easy flowing in heaven! No wonder Hebrews 6:5 calls the gifts of the Spirit:

"the powers of the world [age] **to come."**

Almost without thinking I responded in my thoughts right back to her. "They're not here yet, it's just me right now." She thought back, "OK." And with that she and Tilly turned and bounded away, back over the river and through the grass the way they'd come. As we watched them go, my angel said, "The children really enjoy them."

To be continued...

ABOUT THE AUTHOR

John and Barbara Fenn were born in Kokomo, Indiana, and grew up just a few miles from each other. They attended the same kindergarten, went to many of the same neighborhood birthday parties growing up, and had mutual friends. Barb even attended John's confirmation in the Episcopal Church when they were 12 years old.

They began dating as teenagers and were born again together and baptized with the Holy Spirit at age 16. Each attended Indiana University after graduating high school and were then married in 1978. After graduating from Rhema Bible Training Center in Broken Arrow, Oklahoma in 1980, they moved to the Boulder, Colorado area.

Over the next 12 years, John served in various capacities including Campus Minister at the University of Colorado in Boulder; pastor, associate pastor, and traveling minister. In late 1992 they (and their three sons) moved to Tulsa to become involved with Victory Christian Center, a church of about 10,000 members, Billy Joe and Sharon Daugherty, pastors.

John served as Associate Director of Victory Bible Institute, the Bible school of Victory Christian Center, and then became Executive Director where he served for three years. Resigning in the summer of 2000, he began traveling and teaching in churches and Bible schools all over the country.

In the fall of 2000, Peter Wagner asked John to become the Educational Advisor to the Apostolic Council of Educational Accountability (ACEA), the group of Bible schools around the world affiliated with Peter Wagner and Global Harvest Ministries. He also became a faculty member of the Wagner Leadership Institute (WLI), based out of the World Prayer Center in Colorado Springs, Colorado. (WLI offers Associate, Bachelor, Masters, and Doctorate diplomas granting advanced placement for life and ministry experience.)

In December of 2000, John was asked to become the Canadian National Director for WLI and in March 2001 became the Director of Local Church Seminars, the arm of WLI that takes Wagner Leadership courses into the local church.

In early 2002, John and Barb founded The Church Without Walls International of Tulsa, a house church network, emphasizing relationship-based Christianity.

Pursuing the Seasons of God is John's first book. He has also written *Leaving the Church to Find God*, and contributes to *Ministries Today* magazine. Known for teaching with anointing and by revelation, and flowing with the gifts of the Spirit, his heart's desire is to make known the ways of the Father God.

THE CHURCH WITHOUT WALLS

The Church Without Walls International (CWOW or CWOWI) is dedicated to making disciples of Jesus Christ through the establishment of a network of related house churches around the world.

The seeds of CWOWI were planted in 1992. During a time of prayer the Lord Jesus appeared to John in a visitation and shared some of what he was going to be doing in the future. Part of the Lord's plan was an exodus from many of the 'para-church' organizations that were raised up after the Charismatic renewal of the 1960's and 70's. This would produce a movement of *more* 'para-church' organizations, home prayer meetings, and also home based churches.

At the beginning of 2001, John sought the Lord as to what His next move would be. Having observed the 'hot' revival centers either cooling or getting spiritually off and not seeing anything on the horizon, this was a matter of prayer kept on the 'front burner' before the Lord. John was invited to conduct a seminar and minister at a church of about 200 people in the Toronto, Canada area. During the morning worship service John's eyes were opened to the Spirit realm and he saw Jesus walk over to him, saying in part:

"Do not look at the TV and larger media ministries to try and understand what I am doing in my body today...See what I see: many small churches and ministries investing in relationships, walking in love, pouring their lives into each other; this is where the Spirit is moving today. There is a revolution taking place in my body, a revolution of relationships and discipleships and love. This will affect whole communities and economies.

"...This will be a time of separation within my body. This is the most important point I'm sharing with you today; the true disciples are losing their taste for the shallow and the carnal, and separating themselves from those caught up in the appearance of spirituality....You are part of this move. This move is not a move of the masses, but of the individual. Make disciples, teach the ways of the Spirit, for many are hungry to truly know me, and the Father. Lead them into intimacy and growth in Me. Hear what the Spirit is saying to the church."

The impact of that visitation stayed with John, and by the end of October 2001 he had come to the conclusion that the pattern established in the New Testament of small groups meeting in homes, empowering each other and the Holy Spirit to move and be moved, was the way the Lord intended.

On November 4, 2001, during an evening meeting in a church in Edmonton, Alberta, Jesus appeared again to John. As both John and the host pastor fell to their knees, Jesus laid hands on John and told him to start a home church network 'based on my Word and the things you've learned through the people I've brought across your path this year.' The Lord said he wanted it to be called 'The Church Without Walls International.' The next month, CWOWI began meeting in the Fenn home, and is growing and gaining affiliate house churches at a pace appropriate as relationships develop.

Coming Soon!
The sequel to
Pursuing the Seasons of God

KNOWING THE WAYS OF GOD:
Heaven and Earth as One

In the captivating sequel to *Pursuing the Seasons of God*, John Fenn elaborates on his visitations of the Lord's realm. In *Knowing the Ways of God* John discloses more about his visitations to heaven, which leads to his revelations of the Holy Spirit and God the Father. John also describes ways of holiness as we learn to truly walk in his Presence the whole day.

Since John was a teenager his heart's cry has been Psalm 103:7, "He made known His ways unto Moses; His acts to the children of Israel." John has had a hunger for knowing God's ways—the 'reason behind the reason'—rather than seeing God's acts, the miracles, in his life; for if we know God's ways we will see his acts.

Available Summer 2009 from
Aura Productions LLC and
The Church Without Walls International

Also available from John Fenn:

LEAVING THE CHURCH TO FIND GOD

Motivated by a deep hunger for more of God, millions of Christians are leaving the traditional church to look for more freedom and fulfillment than the routine of five songs, announcements, a plea for money, and a forty-five minute sermon.

Leaving the Church to Find God offers scriptural, safe, and balanced answers, tempered by real life experiences, on how to move from a traditional church structure into meetings that allow the Lord to set the agenda. These new places of worship, outside the four walls of organized church, allow for open ended deep worship that flows from the Holy Spirit, relatable Bible Study and a discussion in which people participate, and strong bonds of fellowship.

$15.00
ISBN: 978-1598583168
First edition 2007

Available from: www.iFaithhome.org/store